Mariane from Papa.

1910.

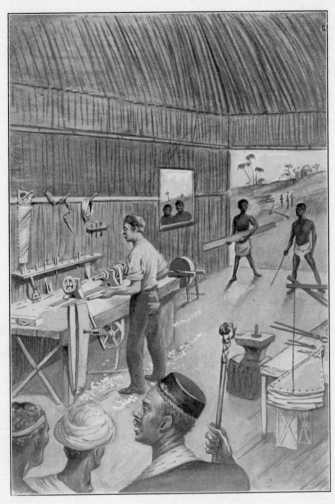

UGANDA'S WHITE MAN OF WORK

UGANDA'S
WHITE MAN OF WORK

A Story of Alexander M. Mackay

SOPHIA LYON FAHS

YOUNG PEOPLE'S MISSIONARY MOVEMENT
OF THE UNITED STATES AND CANADA
NEW YORK   TORONTO

TO THE BOYS AND GIRLS
WHO DELIGHT IN TRUE STORIES OF PEOPLE
AND WHO MAY COME TO REGARD THE WHITE MAN OF
WORK AS ONE OF THE REAL HEROES OF
THEIR ACQUAINTANCE

CONTENTS

ILLUSTRATIONS

PRONUNCIATION OF UGANDA WORDS

The vowels are sounded as follows: a, as a in father; e, as e in they; i, as i in machine; o, as o in note; u, as u in rule. The syllables are given in this list, and have no accent. Number, following word, gives page where word first occurs.

UGANDA WORDS

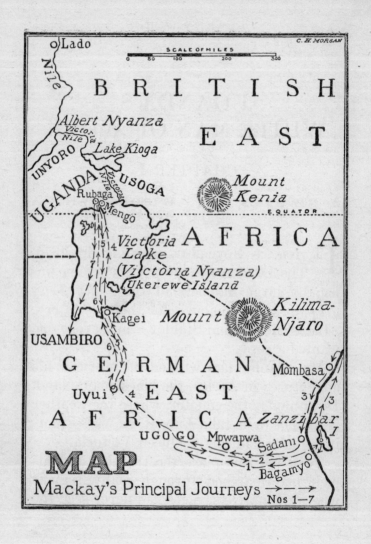

C. H. MORGAN

SCALE OF MILES

0   50   100   200   300

Lado

Nile

B R I T I S H

E A S T

Albert Nyanza

Victoria Nile

Lake Kioga

UNYORO

UGANDA

USOGA

Victoria Nile

Rubaga

Mengo

Mount Kenia

EQUATOR

A F R I C A

Victoria Lake

(Victoria Nyanza)

Ukerewe Island

Kagei

Mount

Kilima-Njaro

USAMBIRO

G E R M A N

Mombasa

Uyui

E A S T

Zanzibar

A F R I C A

UGOGO

Mpwapwa

Sadani

Bagamyo

MAP

Mackay's Principal Journeys ⟶

Nos 1—7

UGANDA'S
WHITE MAN OF WORK

CHAPTER I

A NEWSPAPER MAN'S INTERVIEW WITH A BLACK KING

IT was a November morning in 1875. The London newsboys were selling unusually large numbers of the *Daily Telegraph*. It was enough for the lads to cry, "Latest news from Stanley," and every one wanted a copy.

Mr. Stanley had written the story of his adventures in Africa, the black man's land. Down under the equator, where the weather is too hot to be talked about, he was exploring a lake named for Queen Victoria.

To reach this place the traveler and his men had marched through many regions where the native savages had never seen the

1

face of a white man. Within sound of the roaring of lions and the cries of leopards and hyenas, they had cut their trails through thick African jungles. Their course had led them to face drenching rains and the scorching rays of the tropical sun. Again for days they had plodded along over parched deserts in search of water. At other times they waded more than knee-deep through miry swamps steaming with heat. More than once Mr. Stanley and many of his men had been forced to lie in their tents helpless and burning with fever. Is it strange that a letter from such a correspondent was hailed with enthusiasm in London?

But who had brought the letter all the way to London from Stanley in the heart of Africa? Not a post-office or mail-carrier was to be found within a thousand miles of where Stanley was. The black men had no railroads, or mail-coaches or even roads over which a coach might be pulled. Little wonder then that the letter was seven months old when it appeared in the morning newspaper. When one thinks of the way it came, the marvel is that it ever reached England at all.

It is the story of a pair of boots. A young Frenchman, happening to be with Mr. Stanley at the time, wished to return to Europe. Gladly taking the letter with him, he and his caravan started on their homeward journey. Marching northward along the bank of the River Nile, one day they were suddenly attacked by a band of savage tribesmen. The Frenchman was killed and his corpse was heartlessly left lying unburied on the sand. Later some English soldiers passing by discovered the dead body. Hidden in one of the boots, they found Mr. Stanley's letter. They quickly forwarded it to the English General in Egypt and from there it was sent to the newspaper office in London. Was it by mere chance that the letter was preserved? Some who read the rest of the story may think that perhaps the Great Father who loves both black and white people had something to do with it.

But what had Mr. Stanley written in this letter which all were so eager to read? A message very different from any he had ever sent home before—yes, very different too from that which any one had expected from him. Had he been a missionary, his letter would not have proved so surprising. But Mr. Stanley was an explorer and newspaper correspondent. Indeed, many in England did not know that he even called himself a Christian. Imagine, then, how they felt when they found that part of the letter read something like this:

"King Mutesa of Uganda has been asking me about the white man's God. Although I had not expected turning a missionary, for days I have been telling this black king all the Bible stories I know. So enthusiastic has he become that already he has determined to observe the Christian Sabbath as well as the Mohammedan Sabbath, and all his great captains have con-

4

sented to follow his example. He has further caused the Ten Commandments as well as the Lord's Prayer and the golden commandment of our Saviour, 'Thou shalt love thy neighbor as thyself,' to be written on boards for his daily reading.

"Oh, that some pious, practical missionary would come here! Mutesa would give him anything that he desired—houses, lands, cattle, ivory, and other things. He could call a province his own in one day. It is not the mere preacher, however, that is wanted here. It is the practical Christian, who can teach people how to become Christians, cure their diseases, build dwellings, teach farming, and turn his hand to anything, like a sailor—this is the man who is wanted. Such a one, if he can be found, would become the saviour of Africa.

"Here, gentlemen, is your opportunity—embrace it! The people on the shores of Victoria Lake call upon you. Listen to them. You need not fear to spend money upon this mission, as Mutesa is sole ruler,

5

and will repay its cost tenfold with ivory, coffee, otter skins of a very fine quality, or even in cattle, for the wealth of this country in these products is immense.''

It was not till some time later that Mr. Stanley told all the marvelous tale. No one who heard it wondered any more that he had asked for missionaries to go to Uganda. This is how the story ran:

With his large company of followers, he had begun the voyage northward on Victoria Lake toward Uganda. One clear morning they spied on the far horizon a fleet of canoes coming toward them. As the canoes approached, the white men caught sight of African oarsmen aboard better dressed than any other negroes they had seen in all their journey.

The black sailors hailed the white captain, and when they were near enough to talk with each other, they told him of a strange dream the mother of their king had dreamed two nights before. She thought she saw on the lake a beautiful vessel hav-

6

ing white wings like a bird. On board was a white man with wonderful, large eyes and long black hair. The king, on hearing the dream, had sent these men to find the white man and to invite him to his court. Mr. Stanley could not do other than respond favorably to this royal invitation, and as soon as possible he followed his new guides to the northern shore of the lake, where lay their home country, the kingdom of Uganda.

A great surprise was in store for him when he landed. On the beach stood two thousand people marshaled in two long parallel lines. Noisy salutes from numerous guns, the waving of bright-colored flags, the beating of tom-toms, and the blaring of trumpets, all combined to express their glad welcome. So many Africans all neatly clad in long white robes, with their chiefs arrayed in rich scarlet gowns, made a spectacle new to Mr. Stanley. On his way to Uganda, he had passed through the countries of twenty or more African tribes, but

7

the people were all savages, wearing little or nothing one could call clothes. These Waganda (for that is the name of the people of Uganda), however, seemed to him highly civilized.

The strange white guest was taken to the tent which had been made ready for his coming. Soon a herd of oxen was driven into the courtyard in front of the tent, and then a number of goats and sheep. On the ground a hundred bunches of bananas were piled. By them was laid a queer heap of eatables, including three dozen chickens, four wooden dishes of milk, four baskets of sweet potatoes, fifty ears of green Indian corn, a basket of rice, twenty dozen eggs, and ten pots of Uganda wine—a most generous gift from the king whom the stranger had not yet seen.

When the day came for the white man to visit the king's court, Mr. Stanley with his large company marched along a broad, well-built road leading to the top of a hill, where stood a high, dome-shaped hut built

8

of reed grass. In the doorway of this royal palace stood the tall, slender figure of King Mutesa. His rich, red costume with gold embroidery was very becoming to his graceful, broad-shouldered figure and handsome face. In his talk with Mr. Stanley, he showed himself bright and eager to learn all that he could to increase the greatness of his realm, which was already no small kingdom.

Most African nations were small tribes of a few hundred or thousand people, and most so-called African kings were chiefs over a small group of African villages. The kingdom of Uganda was a most notable exception. Here was a country as large as the New England States, with four million people, all ruled by one powerful monarch. Nor did he rule in the fashon of most African chiefs. His House of Lords met daily in his palace for counsel. These were his great chiefs or earls, who ruled his provinces. He had also his prime minister, his chief judge, his commander-in-chief for the large army of black soldiers, and his grand admiral for the navy of canoes. To the white man, Mutesa seemed like some great Cæsar of Africa.

Mr. Stanley, while still a lad, had told some of his boy friends that when he became a man he was going to be a missionary. This resolve of his boyhood days, however, had slipped from his mind as he became older. Now in Uganda, where he was talking daily with this great African king, there came back to him the longing he had when a boy, and he wished to know how to be a missionary. "If David Livingstone were only alive and here in Uganda," he thought to himself, "what a wonderful work he would do. For should king Mutesa and his millions of subjects become Christians they in turn would make the best kind of missionaries to the savage tribes all about them."

But Mutesa and his people were heathen. This does not mean that they worshiped idols; for had one searched throughout the

10

whole country of Uganda, he probably would not have found a single image. He would have seen, however, here and there along the roadside, usually under the shade of some tree or on the top of a mountain, little huts so small he might have thought they were playhouses for the little Uganda children; but they were used for a very different purpose. To these tiny grass huts the Waganda went to sacrifice.

They believed there was a great god who many hundred years ago created the whole world; but, since men had become very wicked, this god grew angry and would have nothing more to do with the world. It was no use therefore to pray to him, for he would never listen. Instead, they worshiped different kinds of evil spirits. These spirits lived in trees, or on the mountains, or on the lake, or sometimes even in persons; and the Waganda thought they would do much harm unless presents were given to them. Tied to one of the little sacred huts or to a tree beside it might be seen

11

some of these gifts walking around—several sheep or goats or cows. Peeping inside the hut, one might discover also a bunch of bananas or several skin bottles filled with *pombe,* which is a Uganda wine made from bananas. The ugly old man or woman who is guardian of the prayer hut keeps these gifts until the evil spirit is supposed to have taken all he wishes to eat; then the guardian gives himself a treat. So the poor Waganda used to pray to these evil spirits by giving them presents, not of course because they loved the spirits but because they were afraid of them.

There was another religion also, very different from this heathen spirit worship, about which Mutesa had heard a good deal. For about fifty years, Arab merchants had been coming into Uganda to trade calico, wire, beads, and various trinkets for native ivory and slaves.

"There is one true God," these merchants said, "and his greatest prophet is Mohammed. To him God gave great power to do

12

miracles and to conquer many nations. Now, millions upon millions of people worship him. In dreams Mohammed was told by God many wonderful things about heaven and hell, and he has given his followers some good commandments.'' To Mutesa the stories they told of Mohammed seemed far more wonderful than the foolish tales he had heard of the evil spirits in Uganda; and he felt almost like becoming a Mohammedan. He began to wear the Mohammedan dress and turban, he taught his chiefs Mohammedan customs, and he kept the Mohammedan Sabbath. Thus Mr. Stanley found Mutesa half heathen and half Mohammedan, never having heard that to be a Christian was better than either.

Day after day passed, and each day King Mutesa and Mr. Stanley talked together on many subjects. The explorer hesitated to speak of the Christian's God, for he knew not whether Mutesa would be glad or angry to hear of Him. One day at court, when the chiefs were all present, some one of

his own accord asked Mr. Stanley to tell
them of the white man's God. As he began
to tell of God, the loving Father, and of
Jesus Christ, his Son, Mr. Stanley noticed
that the king and courtiers were listening
more intently than he had ever known them
to listen before. Until that day, it had always been thought polite to talk about any
one subject for a short time only; but now
these black men seemed to forget to become
wearied. Each succeeding day, Mr. Stanley continued to talk on this same subject.
His hearers appeared far more interested
in what he said about Jesus than they had
ever been in any of the wonderful things
he had told about civilized people.

Mr. Stanley's visit with Mutesa lasted for
some months. When it became known that
he was soon to leave the country, some one
suggested that at least a few of the things
the white man had said should be written
down so that they would not be forgotten.
By good fortune there were two lads who
together could do the translating and writ-

14

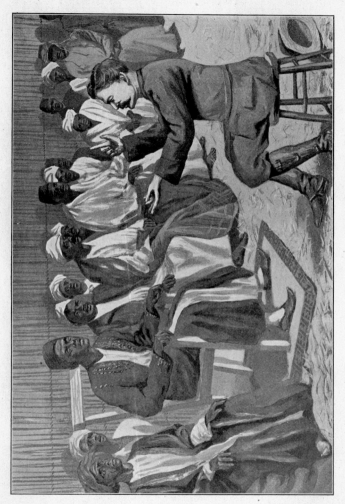

STANLEY TELLS THEM OF THE WHITE MAN'S GOD

ing; one was the king's chief drummer, the other was one of Mr. Stanley's boat boys. So, on thin polished boards of white wood, each about a foot square, they wrote the Ten Commandments and some of the most striking stories of the Old and New Testaments; until the Waganda had a little library of board books.

One memorable day, King Mutesa called to him his chiefs, the officers of his guard, and Mr. Stanley. When all were seated before him, some on the floor and some on stools, in his palace hut, Mutesa began to speak.

"When I became king," he said, in the language of his country, "I delighted in shedding blood because I knew no better. I was only following the customs of my fathers; but, when an Arab trader came and taught me the Mohammedan religion, I gave up the example of my fathers, and beheadings became less frequent. No man can say that since that day he has seen Mutesa drunk with *pombe*. But there were a great

15

many things I could not understand and some things which seemed very unreasonable; but no one in Uganda was able to explain them to me. Now, God be thanked, a white man, Stamlee, has come to Uganda with a book older than the Koran [sacred book] of Mohammed. My boys have read out of it to me, and I find it is a great deal better than the book of Mohammed, besides it is the first and oldest book. The prophet *Musa* [Moses] wrote some of it a long, long time before Mohammed was born. As Kintu, our first king, was a long time before me, so *Musa* was before Mohammed. Now I want you, my chiefs and soldiers, to tell me what we shall do. Shall we believe in *Isa* [Jesus] and *Musa* or in Mohammed?"

One of the group, Chambarango by name, spoke up: "Let us take that which is the best."

"But," came a reply from the prime minister, "we do not know which is the best. The Arabs say their book is the best, and the white men say their book is the best—

16

how then can we know which speaks the truth?"

Then Kauta, the king's steward, said: "When Mutesa became a son of Mohammed, he taught me, and I became one; if my master says he taught me wrong, having got more knowledge, he can now teach me right. I am waiting to hear his words."

Pleased at this, Mutesa again addressed his chiefs: "Kauta speaks well. If I taught him how to become a Mohammedan, I did it because I believed it to be good. Chambarango says, 'Let us take that which is best.' True, I want that which is the best, and I want the true book; but the *katikiro* [prime minister] asks, 'How are we to know which is true?' And I will answer him. Listen to me. The Arabs and the white men behave exactly as they are taught in their books, do they not? The Arabs come here for ivory and slaves, and we have seen that they do not always speak the truth, and that they buy men of their own color and treat them badly, putting them in chains and beating

17

them. The white men, when offered slaves, refuse them, saying, 'Shall we make our brothers slaves? No; we are all sons of God.' I have not heard a white man tell a lie yet. Speke came here, behaved well, and went his way home with his brother Grant. [Speke and Grant were earlier explorers in Africa.] They bought no slaves, and the time they were in Uganda they were very good. Stamlee came here, and he would take no slaves. What Arab would have refused slaves like these white men? Though we deal in slaves, it is no reason why it should not be bad; and when I think that the Arabs and the white men do as they are taught, I say that the white men are greatly superior to the Arabs, and I think, therefore, that their book must be a better book than Mohammed's, and of all that Stamlee has read from this book I see nothing too hard for me to believe. I have listened to it all well pleased, and now I ask you, shall we accept this book or Mohammed's book as our guide?''

18

Seeing clearly just what the king wanted, they all answered, "We will take the white men's book."

Thus it was that Mutesa announced himself a follower of the Christ and the Christian's Book. He promised to build a church, and begged that other white men might come to teach him and his people about the good way.

"Stamlee," he said, "say to the white people, when you write to them, that I am like a man sitting in darkness, or born blind, and that all I ask is that I may be taught how to see, and I shall continue a Christian while I live."

Such an appeal Mr. Stanley could not let pass unheeded, and the letter was written to the *Daily Telegraph*.

But the newspaper correspondent had asked a very hard thing. London folk had heard before of King Mutesa of Uganda. Two earlier travelers had told very different stories of this great heathen monarch. Which was to be believed? They had said that in Mutesa's court a fair trial was never known. If one of the king's chiefs failed to salute his majesty properly, his head was in danger. If his bark cloth dress was not tied over his right shoulder according to the proper fashion, Mutesa was likely to order the man to be put to death. In an instant every one near the offender would rise, drums would be beaten, drowning the man's cries for mercy, and the unfortunate victim would be dragged off to his fate. Even the king's three or four hundred wives lived in daily fear of death by order of their master. Such was the king who Stanley was now saying wanted Christian teachers. Who knew but that he might not soon tire of white men too, and order their lives also to be taken?

Then, too, the young men of England thought of the long and dangerous journey across a country with no railroads. They thought of the wild animals, of the deadly hot climate, and of the savage and cannibal chiefs through whose countries they would

20

pass. They pictured the loneliness of living so many months away from all their white friends and loved ones. What joy would there be in living in a small grass hut with mud floors and no windows? Why should any man, who might some day be an honored clergyman in a peaceful town in England, go to this uncivilized land and be his own butcher, baker, and candlestick-maker?

Was there even one man in England who would take Mr. Stanley's letter seriously? Would any one be willing to leave home and friends and risk his life just because a black king in the heart of Africa, plotting perhaps for the white man's life, had asked for a missionary?

Moreover one man could not go alone. A number of men would have to be found who would go in a party. Thousands of dollars would be needed for traveling expenses alone. Was this undertaking worth all it might cost? What would come of Mr. Stanley's letter?

21

CHAPTER II

IN an office in Salisbury Square in London a small group of men read Mr. Stanley's newspaper letter. They were men who had been chosen to gather the money given for missions by the churches and to send out missionaries. They were called secretaries of the Church Missionary Society.

"Is there anything we can do for King Mutesa," they said to one another? "If he is truly longing to be taught about God, will it not be a crime to refuse to send some one to tell him? Even if he is not sincere, ought we not to act as if he were? But who has the heart to ask any young man to go? And who would be willing to give money for the undertaking?"

22

Discouraged by the difficulties they saw, yet unwilling to drop the matter carelessly, they locked the office doors and knelt together to ask the Father to tell them what He wanted them to do. Not long did they wait for an answer to their prayers. The third day after Mr. Stanley's article was published, a letter came addressed to Mr. Hutchinson, Secretary of the Church Missionary Society, which showed that some one else had the needs of Uganda in mind.

"Dear Mr. Hutchinson," it read, "Often have I thought of the people in the interior of Africa in the region of Uganda, and I have longed and prayed for the time to come when the Lord would open the door so that heralds of the gospel might enter the country. The appeal of Stanley to the Christian Church from Mutesa's capital, seems to show that the time has come for the soldiers of the cross to make an advance into that region. If the Committee of the Church Missionary Society are prepared at once and with energy to start a mission to

Victoria Lake, I shall gladly give you £5,000 [about $25,000] with which to begin.

"I desire to be known in this matter only as
    'An Unprofitable Servant.'
        (Luke xvii.10).''

The hearts of the committeemen beat fast as they read the letter through. It all seemed so wonderful. "God must be in this," they said to one another, "God must be in this. He must have touched the heart of Mutesa and made him want to ask for missionaries: he must have told Stanley to send the plea on to England: and he must have put it in the heart of this Christian man of wealth, whose name we do not know, to make this generous gift. Who are we that we should stand back and say to God, 'No, we are afraid to do our part to help.' ''

They began to study their geographies, and to read magazine articles and books of travel that told about Uganda and the way to go there. By the time a week of such thought and prayer had passed, they decided

24

that they would send letters to different newspapers asking for men and money. Soon another gift of £5,000 [$25,000] was made. This encouraged them to work and pray for even more. How glad they were, not many days later, when they found that the sum of £24,000 in all [$120,000] was ready to be used!

These, however, were not the only letters which came to make them glad. Some were from men who had no money to give, but who wanted to give their lives. One was from a retired officer of the British navy, Lieutenant G. Shergold Smith. One was from an Irish architect, Mr. O'Neill; another, from a minister, the Rev. Mr. Wilson; another from Mr. Clark, an engineer; and another from Mr. William Robertson, an artisan; and still another from Dr. John Smith, a physician of Edinburgh. All these men wanted to go, and the secretaries at the office said they would be glad to send them. Another, however, a carpenter, Mr. James Robertson, they refused to send because of his poor health; but, having already sold out his business, he said he would go and pay his own expenses. These seven men, with one other, made up the party who in answer to Stanley's newspaper appeal sailed a few months later for Mutesa's land.

This other was the youngest of them all —a Scotchman named Alexander Mackay. [He pronounced his name, Mack-i.] He wrote from Germany where he was gaining a reputation for himself as one of the head men in an important machine factory. His business was to draw plans for large engines.

Even when a boy, Alexander had always been fond of machinery. Living in a little Scottish village, when a lad of about twelve years, he used often to walk four miles to the nearest railway station and four miles back just to see the engine puff into town hauling a train of cars, stop a minute or two, and then steam off again. His good-natured fun made him a great favorite at the village blacksmith's, at the gas works, the carding-mill, and the carpenters' shops. Often he would visit these places, for he liked to watch the men and the machinery as they did their work.

While he was at grammar-school in a larger town, he could almost never be induced to go on holiday excursions with the other lads. Instead, he would slip away to a photographer's where he would learn how to use a camera, or he would find his way to the shipyards to watch the builders as they covered the steel ribs with timbers, placed the masts, and sewed the rigging for fishing schooners. During his college course, too, those studies were most to his liking in which he could make something with his hands.

His father wanted him to be a clergyman, but the boy did not favor the suggestion. He was, however, a true Christian. The thought of going as a missionary to some heathen land came to him when a child. His father used to talk with him about the new discoveries in Central Africa, and his mother often told him stories about missionaries.

More than a year before Mr. Stanley's plea was published, Mackay had read an appeal for Christian doctors to go to Madagascar. Although he knew that thousands of Christians on that island had suffered death as martyrs, he purposed, if it seemed to be God's wish for him to do so, to go to Madagascar as an "engineering missionary." By this he meant that he wanted to go to that uncivilized island to teach the natives to build roads, bridges, railways, to work mines, and to learn to use various kinds of machinery, and so help them to become more useful Christians. A strange sort of missionary, you say. This is what many of his friends thought, too; for they had never before heard of a mechanic becoming a missionary; but it did not change Mackay's purpose. He began at once to prepare for his work by studying the language of the people of Madagascar.

This plan, however, was changed for a better one. On a bitter cold night, during the Christmas holidays of 1875, he finished reading Stanley's book, *How I Found Livingstone.* Laying the book on the table, he noticed an old copy of the Edinburgh *Daily Review.* His eyes fell on the words "Henry Wright, Honorary Secretary, Church Missionary Society." His curiosity was at once awakened. He had found one of the appeals sent out by the secretaries in London asking for men to go out as missionaries to Mutesa's kingdom. Mr. Mackay, then and there, although it was after midnight, wrote to Mr. Wright offering to go to help teach Mutesa's people how to be useful Christians.

"My heart burns for the deliverance of Africa," he wrote, "and if you can send me to any one of these regions which Livingstone and Stanley have found to be groaning under the curse of the slave-hunter I shall be very glad!"

So it all came about that in the quiet, old committee-room of the Church Missionary

29

House one April day the eight young men bound for Uganda said good-by to the committeemen who stayed at home. One of the secretaries, speaking for the rest, gave the young men their last instructions. Then each of the party replied in his turn. Mr. Mackay being the youngest was the last to speak.

"There is one thing," he said, "which my brethren have not said, and which I want to say. I want to remind the committee that within six months they will probably hear that one of us is dead." He paused, and there was a solemn stillness in the room. Then, he went on: "Yes; is it at all likely that eight Englishmen should start for Central Africa, and all be alive six months after? One of us, at least—it may be I— will surely fall before that. But," he added, "what I want to say is this; when the news comes, do not be cast down, but send some one else immediately to take the vacant place."

By the end of April all the party had

30

sailed. The good-bys were hard to say. Friends, mothers, fathers, brothers, sisters, and, for some, their wives and children, they might never see again. Yet their gladness was more than their sorrow as the steamship put out to sea. They believed that the Heavenly Father was their pilot. He had raised the money. He had called his workers, and they were now going with him.

Five long weeks at sea! Then down by the equator a few miles off the east coast of Africa, the voyagers at last sighted the island of Zanzibar. There in the city of Zanzibar, the busiest seaport in East Africa, they landed.

But the kingdom of Mutesa lay about a thousand miles beyond. By foot or on donkey's back, they must travel through a wild tropical country for a distance as far as from Washington to Chicago. Even then the next to the largest lake in all the world —and a very stormy and treacherous one it is, too,—would still separate them from Mutesa's land.

31

In these days of railroads and telegraphs,
it is difficult to understand how hard it was
in 1876 to prepare for a journey of one
thousand miles into the interior of Africa.
On leaving the coast, the missionaries would
say good-by to stores of every kind. Nothing could be purchased at any price in the
country through which they would march
except food such as the black men ate,
elephants' tusks, animal skins, bark cloth,
and slaves. Even these could not be bought
with silver and gold or with paper money.
African chiefs would insist on bead money
and on such things as red caps, handkerchiefs, cloth, wire, guns, and gunpowder for
pay.

Before setting sail from Liverpool, the
missionaries had spent weeks in hurrying
to and fro from store to store. They had
ordered books, clothing, medicines, hammers, nails, spades, saws, hatchets, axes,
chisels, a forge and bellows, shovels, grind-
stones, a pump. These do not cover half the
list. Perhaps the most unique articles in

their outfit, were a printing-press, a magic lantern, a music-box and a steam launch.

Much of the bulkiest baggage was left to be purchased in Zanzibar. No trudging around, however, from store to store this time. As soon as the news spread about the town that a party of Britishers had arrived bound for Victoria Lake, merchants from India and Arabs began to call on them. A list of the articles needed was carefully made out and the goods ordered.

After several days, there came to the house where the missionaries were staying, a number of half-naked Indian coolies. In one of the houses surrounding the courtyard, they stacked scores of bundles of varied shapes and sizes. First, came boxes of dried foods, pans, kettles, and dishes. Most of the camping outfit was purchased in Zanzibar, including tents, white umbrellas, waterproof sheets, blankets, cots, and stools.

The largest bundles of all, however, were filled with African money. By the door were lying piles of small change—handkerchiefs and red caps. Over in one corner, the coolies were rolling $50 bills—bales of colored and striped cotton cloth. Then came the bead money—bags of large beads and small beads, oval beads and round beads, some blue, some red, some green, and some white. At last, the coolies, panting with heat, lugged in the heaviest bundles of all— huge coils of brass wire—thousands and thousands of yards. Handkerchiefs, red caps, cloth, beads, and brass wire, together weighing hundreds of pounds, were all to be used as money.

The baggage being collected, the next problem was how to get it carried across the country to Mutesa's kingdom. Having nothing but crooked narrow trails for roadways, the missionaries were obliged to travel as the Arabs had always done before them. This meant picking their way on foot single file, mile after mile, and using black men as beasts of burden.

Now, even sturdy black baggage-carriers will not march with a burden on their heads

34

weighing more than about sixty pounds. So all the white men's freight had to be taken from trunks and boxes and repacked. The boxes were opened, their contents spread out on the ground in piles of the size and weight of one man's load. Then shaping each pile, if possible, into the form of a large pillow-bolster, they wrapped it in several thicknesses of cloth and tied it tightly with strong rope. When neither rain nor rough handling could harm what was within the wrappings, the bundles were ready for the heads of the African porters.

While some of the missionary band were busy packing supplies, others were toiling at perhaps the hardest work of all. Trudging from hut to hut in the negro quarter of Zanzibar, they were hiring baggage-carriers. Others having crossed the channel to the mainland were plodding about from village to village working at the same trying task; for as many as five hundred porters were needed. For many weeks this search dragged along. Finally, it was decided to divide the missionary party into four caravans, so that some could begin the march before all of the five hundred baggage-carriers were found.

Two of the caravans had not yet started when the "angel of death" visited the camp. "Within six months you will probably hear that one of us is dead," Mr. Mackay had said to the committee before leaving England. Within four months the prophecy was fulfilled. On a little island off the coast, a grave was dug for the body of James Robertson, the carpenter, who had gone with the party at his own expense. He had given his life for a king and a people he had never seen.

The next to the last caravan to leave the coast was Mr. Mackay's. Crowds of people from the town of Bagamoyo flocked to see the white man and his procession file out of the village. A bugle call had summoned those hired for the journey to gather before the white man's quarters. A man's load was given to each carrier and his place

The Procession Files Out of the Village

in the procession assigned. First marched a half-dozen soldiers, who never had even carried guns until Mr. Mackay began to train them. Then came the leader of the porters with a load on his shoulders twice as heavy as any one else carried. He was followed by about two hundred men loaded with their sixty pound pillow-bolsters. Behind them, straggled the wives of a few porters, an aged father, and a handful of small boys. Next walked a line of four donkeys laden with parts of a steam launch, other machinery and tools, and much of the cloth.

After them, marched Mr. Hartwell, a sailor, who was now Mr. Mackay's only white companion. He was followed by a cook, Mr. Mackay's personal servant, three stoker boys, an interpreter, an African mason, and a carpenter. Last of all came a group of soldiers, Mr. Mackay, and a dog. It was an interesting procession for the townspeople to watch, for marching single file, they stretched along the path for about a quarter of a mile.

Talking, laughing, and singing, the long line wound here and there through the tall jungle grass, down some little valley or up a tiny hill. But the sun shone hot above them, and the path was hard and dry. In an hour or so, the heat became oppressive. The orderly line grow irregular. Some straggled behind, blaming Mr. Mackay for their discomfort. Those accustomed to march walked steadily on toward a river about three miles distant where they knew they could rest, but some of the inexperienced ones were already lying flat on the ground crying for water and bewailing that they had ever been such fools as to leave their homes.

During the first few days, the caravan proceeded very slowly. The men insisted on marching only an hour or two in the morning and on resting all the next day. By promising higher wages if they would march longer each day, Mr. Mackay succeeded in getting them to march from sunrise or soon after until about noon.

38

The country through which they passed varied greatly from day to day. Sometimes they pushed their way through fields of grass as tall as themselves or even higher and having stalks almost as thick as sugarcane. Every now and then they were startled by a hippopotamus or an antelope scared from its hiding-place in the heavy grass.

Starting off again, they came to a swamp more beautiful to look at than to wade through. It was filled with large graceful ferns and beautiful pink flowers. At night it was alive with fireflies. The missionaries thought this sight worth going hundreds of miles to see. They also passed through fields of millet growing to a height of sixteen or eighteen feet. At another place, they were refreshed by the cool shade of a park-like forest. The giant cacti and euphorbia trees made it seem very different from the woodlands at home. They discovered gorgeous butterflies and many birds of brilliant plumage that their friends in England had never seen. Sometimes the forest changed to jungle. Then with an ax and hatchet foot by foot they had to slash a wider path in front of them, before the donkeys could wedge their way between the two walls of underbrush on either side.

You would have enjoyed seeing how Mr. Mackay fed his large family of two hundred blacks. Reaching a place near a water supply where it was planned that the caravan would spend the night, tents were pitched and the goods piled under a tree or in a tent. When in a district where wild beasts were common, a fence of thorns was built round the camp. As soon as this work was completed, the head men of the caravan collected before Mr. Mackay's tent and cried *"Posho, Bwana"* ["Rations, **Master.**"] Instead of handing out food to them, he had a bale of calico brought to him and, measuring it by the length of the forearm from the elbow to the tip of the middle finger, he gave each one eight of these lengths for every sixteen men of whom he had charge.

40

With these pieces of calico for money these men went to the natives of the place and bought their own food.

"To be a father to such a large family of children," wrote Mr. Mackay, "every day crying out *'Posho!'* which means, 'Give us our daily bread,' is by no means a joke. Their little disputes and complaints I have to settle. My interpreter is poor in English and sometimes says just the opposite of what I mean. Still we get on wonderfully well."

Water at times was harder to find than food. More than once the caravan was obliged to set up camp and with empty water-bottles to walk forth in seach of something with which to quench their thirst. When no spring could be found, the natives would dig holes in the ground which would usually fill with a muddy looking liquid resembling soap-suds. With such as this blacks and whites alike had to be content.

Fortunately, Mr. Mackay had very few sick men to take care of. In a caravan a little in front of his, smallpox was raging severely, and here and there along the road lay the bodies of men who had died on the march. In order to escape the tracks of this caravan, Mr. Mackay left the regular road and for two days he and his men waded knee-deep through a mixture of black mud and water.

Through his attempt to hustle the slow-going African, Mr. Mackay overtaxed himself and was taken sick with the African fever. For a few days he was too weak to walk and was obliged to ride one of the donkeys that had been carrying baggage. At last, however, the feverish coast-plains were left behind. Gladly they climbed the mountains to the little town of Mpwapwa. They had traveled only a little farther than from New York to Boston; yet the march had dragged along for six weeks.

At Mpwapwa three of the missionary caravans met. For a few days the white men rested and prepared for the journey ahead. How they enjoyed their after-dinner chats

as they sat together in one of the tents telling the experiences of the march!

Only a few days at Mpwapwa and then
two of the caravans are off again—made up
of Dr. Smith, Mr. Mackay, and over three
hundred baggage-carriers. By their first
Sunday, they overtook another of the caravans ahead, led by Lieutenant Smith, the
old naval officer.

For thirty or forty miles beyond them
stretched a dreary plateau covered with a
thick, low jungle. Not a human being lived
in all this lonely forest and the caravan
could find neither food nor water except
what they carried with them in knapsacks
and water-bottles. After days of this tire-
some march, they entered the wide, open
land of Ugogo. Here every few miles was
a new village; and with every group of villages they found a new chief. Each chief
insisted that to travel through his country
was a privilege, and the white man would
have to pay for it. The paying of this toll,
or *honga* as they call it, added not only a

great deal of expense to caravan-travel, but also caused many annoying delays.

Their experience with one of the chiefs of Ugogo will show something of the manner in which they were treated in many villages. A short distance from the chief's village, the caravan encamped. The following morning two of the more intelligent Africans were sent to call on the chief, and to take him a gift of some cloth. They found a monarch much soiled with dirt and grease sitting on a stool in his wattled hut drinking *pombe*. He received the cloth, but demanded a great deal more. Fifty cloths, he insisted was none too much. The messengers claimed that such a demand was robbery and hour after hour they quarreled with him. At nightfall the messengers returned to camp and reported, "The chief is sitting at *pombe,* and won't hear reason. He says, 'The white man is a great sultan in his own country, and he must pay a big *honga.*'"

The next morning, they returned to the

mud palace and again tried to reason with
the stubborn chief. Later in the day, Lieutenant Smith himself entered his majesty's
presence and added his word of protest.
Finally the chief agreed to receive forty-
five bales of cloth.

The troublesome matter being settled,
Lieutenant Smith thought he would enter-
tain the chief with some of the white man's
wonders. Taking a match box from his
pocket, he struck a light. The chief was
frightened, or pretended to be, and cried,
"The white man is trying to kill me!"
Rushing from his hut, he disappeared.
Later he sent to the missionaries' camp to
say that for such a serious offense they
would have to pay as a forfeit twenty-five
bales of cloth more than had already been
given.

So the privilege of camping for three days
in this chief's realm, cost the missionaries
seventy bales of cloth or about $100.
When the cloth was paid the big drum of the
village was beaten and the caravan knew

that they were at liberty to proceed on their way.

On entering Ugogo, Mr. Mackay's fever had returned and for miles he had to be carried in a hammock. There being good water in the land of this ruler he would like to have stayed longer in his domain. He feared however, that more *honga* would be charged him if he remained.

What should he do? Just beyond, lay a nine days' wilderness and immediately after that was another that would take three days to cross. No water and no food were to be found in these jungles, and the caravan's supply of provisions was very low. Lieutenant Smith and Dr. Smith urged him to return to the coast. Hard as it was to turn back, Mr. Mackay finally yielded to the counsel of his friends.

Lying in a hammock swung from the shoulders of two strong men Mr. Mackay was carried back to the town of Mpwapwa over the path by which he had just come. Eight others carried his tent, instruments, clothes, cooking utensils, and some cloth with which to buy food.

At one time, he became so weak that he expected to die. Calling for a writing desk, he mixed an ink powder and commenced what he thought would be his last letter on earth. But during the night, a change for the better came. Mr. Mackay said a bunch of home letters had been his best medicine. In eleven days he walked the entire distance from Mpwapwa to the coast, and on reaching Zanzibar he was almost a well man.

It was now the last of November, 1876. One year had passed since Mr. Stanley's letter had appeared in the *Daily Telegraph.* A band of eight young men from Great Britain had started for Mutesa's land. One had laid down his life at the very gateway of the continent. One having started inland had been stricken with fever and was obliged to begin the march anew. One had settled at Mpwapwa to start a mission there. The other five with their hundreds of black carriers were plodding along through jungle

47

and swamp and over mountain and plain toward Victoria Lake.

But what of King Mutesa? Since "Stam-lee" left, no word had come from the white men. Were they going to leave him "sitting in darkness"? When would they ever come to teach him "how to see"?

CHAPTER III

JUNGLE ROADS, OX-CARTS, AND FLY BITES

SINCE Mr. Mackay landed in Zanzibar six months had come and gone. And what had he accomplished? A three hundred mile march inland only to be made all over again! A new outfit must now be purchased; a new caravan of porters must be hired; and again they must pick their way over the same rough, narrow trail. Weary as Mr. Mackay was of this snail-like way of traveling, he set to work immediately to prepare for a second caravan journey.

But a letter from England changed his plans. The secretaries there, having heard of Mackay's sickness, wrote that he must not begin the march into the interior until June, when the rainy season would be over. In the meantime, they said he might see what

49

could be done about building a road to
Mpwapwa. At first this man of energy was
disappointed. When again would he see his
friends, he thought, and how much longer
must he wait before telling King Mutesa of
the white man's God? Yet, without a complaint, he was ready to turn road-builder.

But his friends up-country sorely needed
fresh supplies. At the earliest possible moment, he must gather a caravan and, with
some one else at its head, he must send it off
toward Victoria Lake. The story is again
one of delays and hardships. Compelled to
sail three hundred miles north from Zanzibar to find porters, he tramped back on foot
from village to village along the coast.
What discomforts were crowded into the
three months he spent hiring baggage-carriers, no one but Mr. Mackay himself knew!

Writing of one of his long journeys, he
said: "This walk was much harder than
any I have made before. Days of man-
grove swamp, hours of wading nearly to the
waist, and occasional swimming across rapid

rivers usually gave me an appetite for food and rest. I had only a man (my cook) and a boy with me, so that I had to dispense with the luxuries of a tent, bed, change of clothing, and such things. I often got a hut to sleep in, but when not, I enjoyed sleeping in the open air, preferring it often to a cow-stable swarming with ants and similar unpleasant friends."

Later he wrote again: "I have slept in all sorts of places—a cow-stable, a sheep-cote, a straw hut not much larger than a dog-kennel, a hen-house, and often in no house at all. So anything suits me, provided I get a spot tolerably clear of ants and mosquitoes. Of all the plagues of Egypt, none could have been worse than that of the black ants!"

Finally, the carriers were hired and the caravan was started on its way toward Victoria Lake. The young missionary, however, who had gathered it was again helplessly ill with fever. The strain of the three months of labor had proved too much for him. Had it not been for the kind nursing of white friends in Zanzibar his life story would perhaps have ended here.

Six weeks later, however, he was out of bed and enthusiastic over the commonplace labor of building a road. Having hired forty black carriers, besides women to carry loads and men to drive donkeys, he set up a camp about five miles from the coast on the top of a hill overlooking a small town. This seemed a most desirable spot for camping because it was high and exposed to fresh breezes from both the sea and the land. Here Mr. Mackay planned to live several weeks, while working on the road in the neighborhood.

Writing from this camp, he said: "I sit at present like Abraham in his tent door. My servants, my flocks, and my herds are about me. I am well again, thank God, and camp life has set my spirits up. My horse, my dog, my goat, my oxen, and donkeys, with all my household of nearly seventy men and women, are enough to feed, and quite enough to look after at one time.

52

"My working gang consists of only about forty men, and these I have armed with the best American axes, English hatchets, picks and spades and saws. All these tools are as new to them as they are to the natives of the villages we pass through. A donkey's load of large iron nails I have taken with me, and plenty of hammers, but the wood is as a rule too hard for the iron to enter. For such cases, I have supplied myself with a large stock of strong rope of cocoanut fiber.

"One of the tools I brought with me from England proves more serviceable than all the rest together. It is merely a two-foot grindstone which I have mounted on a wooden frame. Every evening when we return from work in time, the edges of the tools are applied to the face of this wonderful machine, while the villagers crowd around as anxiously gazing on as little Toddy ever did when he wanted 'to see the w'eels go wound.'"

During the morning hours the gang would be busy with axes, saws, and shovels. In the open and level country, men would be scattered here and there over the trails, each clearing and leveling his own particular stretch of the road. Perhaps far behind the rest, would be five or six workmen toiling steadily at some unusually sturdy tree, whose hard wood was too much for the saws and axes.

In the dense jungles, on the other hand, the men would be huddled together like colonies of ants, doing their hardest work. So thick were some of these woodlands that the black toilers were often hidden from sight. According to Mr. Mackay even a cat could scarcely find room to wedge its way through the matted underbrush, creepers, and tropical ferns. Where a narrow trail had before been cut through these miles of jungle, the branches and hanging vines were so closely interlaced overhead that the traveler could scarcely get a glimpse of the blue sky, and would be walking, as it were, through a damp, leafy tunnel. To saw through a tree-trunk in such a tangled mass, seldom meant that the tree would fall, unless the matted undergrowth were first slashed away.

Sometimes they shelved out a footing around the brow of a mountain; sometimes they had to cover swampy stretches with layers of logs, thus making a corduroy road. At other times they prepared to ford streams by grading the banks on either side.

Their greatest achievement was the building of a bridge in seven days. The ignorant black men had never before seen any kind of a bridge for wagon traffic. The entire structure was built of wood almost as hard as iron so that Mr. Mackay thought that it would long stand against the attacks of white ants.

These negro laborers, like most of their race, worked best when singing. As they chopped and shoveled and dug, one might have heard them chant this song made up for Mr. Mackay's special benefit:

> *"Eh, eh, muzungu mbaya,*
> *Tu kati miti,*
> *Twende Ulaya."*

55

Put into English it means:

Is not the white man very bad,
He fells to the ground the tall trees,
To make a way for the Englishman.

Days, weeks, and even months came and
went. All the way black men slashed and
sawed, and dug and leveled, while Mr.
Mackay rode or walked back and forth
among them, encouraging them to their
best work. Ofttimes he showed them what
to do and how to do it by taking shovel or
pick in hand and leveling banks, or filling
mud-holes. He provided their food, planned for their shelter and cared for their
sick. He longed to be able to talk their
language that he might tell them of the
God who cared for them and wanted them
to live useful lives. Finally, after one hundred days of vigorous toil, the road was
completed.

Before it was begun there was only a
crooked, narrow trail stretching for the two
hundred and thirty miles to Mpwapwa. At
some places, donkeys could scarcely be

pulled through the thick jungle; porters tore their scanty clothes or cut their skins on the thorny bushes; and for lack of room over-head, bales of cotton had to be dragged along the ground. When they finished the work, there was a clear road all the way from the coast to the mountains and it was broad enough to allow the largest ox-carts to pass each other at any point.

The natives of the country were half pleased and half alarmed because of this wondrous achievement. Mr. Mackay wrote: "Passers-by open their mouths as well as their eyes at the *njia kubwa* [big road] of the white man; and when they return to talk together at evening in their villages, the story of the 'big road' is told, and, as is always the case in Africa, with enormous exaggerations. To the chief men, however, the story is not always pleasing; and the report is being widely spread that the English are coming to take possession of the country. The chief of the village near which I made the bridge, took a more practical view of the matter, and told me one day, with all the command his dirty visage could assume, that I must pay a hundred dollars for cutting down the trees in his territory. I told him that it was he who should give me the hundred dollars, to pay my men for making a bridge which he and his people could not make. For as soon as I was gone, he would call it his own, and probably levy *honga* from those caravans which cared to pay him."

When the road was completed, Mr. Mackay and his men returned to the coast. "Now," he thought, "we are ready to travel in a civilized way. We will buy oxen and carts for carrying our baggage and we will reach Mpwapwa in half the time it took us before. The experiment has been tried most successfully in South Africa by other men; why cannot we succeed in Central Africa?"

Most enthusiastically he began preparations for the journey, but again he found that he had a difficult task before him. In the first place, oxen, which never before had been hitched to carts, had to be broken in. Neither could men be found who had ever before driven oxen, so that new hands had to be taught. This was harder, Mr. Mackay said, than to teach the oxen to pull.

Then, too, they were obliged to camp in a very unhealthful place. Up in his old camp on the hill, many of the oxen died from the poisonous sting of the tsetse fly, and Mr. Mackay with his men and flocks and herds was obliged to move to the plain. For at least two months before they started on their journey, it rained nearly every day. The plain became a quagmire and the training of oxen and men had to stop.

Waiting so long at the coast for the rainy season to pass, Mr. Mackay's men grew discontented and unruly and some of them deserted him. Also, Mr. Tytherleigh, his assistant who had lately arrived from England, was laid low with a severe attack of fever. They must soon travel along or many others also would be sick.

In spite of the rain and mud, therefore,

59

the long lumbering caravan moved out of the town. There were six large awkward carts loaded to the full with baggage. Teams of from eight to twenty oxen were pulling each cart. Many more oxen were taken as reserves to fill the places of those which might be injured or become sick on the road. In all there were as many as eighty oxen. To drive and to lead these animals and to manage the brakes on the carts required thirty men, and thirty more might have been seen carrying on their heads bundles of baggage. Behind the carts came a flock of sheep and goats, to be used as food for the party, and also five donkeys and six dogs.

Over each cart waved a flag. When they camped by the road for the night, a flag waved also above each tent door, the largest of all flying over Mr. Mackay's tent. These were not the national flags of Great Britain or of the United States; they were blue, each with a large red cross painted on its center. The African heathen could not understand what they meant, but any Christian will readily guess the meaning of the flags.

After ten days of travel, Mr. Mackay tells this story of their adventures: "A long time without practise, on account of the rain and mud, had put the oxen out of trim, so that when we set off we were able to make only a few hundred yards' progress the first day. Next day more rain made matters worse, and we made not half a mile. I then resolved to remove four hundred pounds of baggage from each cart. After a couple of days' rearranging loads, we got a fair start, but another deluge of rain caused us to stop short at the foot of the hill where our old camp had been. Next day we got to the top of the hill, and have since then made a little progress when it was fair.

"After ten marching days, usually with double teams in each cart, and wheels down to the axle in mud, we are camped to-day only ten miles from the coast. I have resolved, therefore, to send back two of the larger carts with their loads."

About two weeks later [Christmas Day, 1877] he wrote again: "You should see me every day with clothes bespattered with mud and hands black like a chimney-sweep's catching the spokes of the wheels every now and then as they get into holes, and yelling at the top of my voice to the oxen, till the forest resounds. So much yelling have I to do in the six hours we march a day, that when I get into camp I am always quite hoarse. A team of twenty-six oxen, frequently spanned on in front of one cart, does need good shouting and lashing to get them to pull together. It is not walking with my umbrella or riding on a donkey behind a cart, but ever getting some one or other or all the carts out of this difficulty and the next. My men are far from skilful in the art of driving long teams through the forest, and are constantly bringing the carts against trees or stones or into holes, not infrequently upsetting them altogether. It is hopeless, for instance, in trying to cross a river, to find one ox lie down, another break loose and run away, several more with their faces to the cart, where their tails should be, and so on. One's patience gets sorely tried by such occurrences, but the only way is patiently to arrange all and try again."

Here are some lines from another letter: "A terrible scorpion crawled over me just now. I should like you to see half the horrors of the kind I see in a day—snakes and ants on the ground below till one shudders from top to toe, and terrible biting, stinging, huge flies all above and about, drawing blood at every bite. Last night I was busy sleeping, when just at my ear a terrible growl of a hyena made me spring to my feet, seize my rifle and fire; but 'Bobby,' my dog, was before me, and set up such a furious bark that the beast skulked off before I had time to present it with a bullet. I dare say you think it a dastardly kind of life, to lie with a revolver under one's pillow and a rifle at one's side, but it is necessary here, for anything may happen at any moment, and it is best to be ready."

Sometimes Mr. Mackay's experiences were more amusing than dangerous. One night he was sleeping soundly on a mattress on the floor of his tent, when he was awakened by a very uncomfortable feeling of numerous things crawling over him. To his surprise he found a colony of brown ants in his tent. Unwittingly he had camped across their line of march. By thousands they were crawling over him and his mattress. He climbed on top of a box, while some of his men set fire to the whole ground inside and around his tent. After an hour's struggle, the ants disappeared, but Mr. Mackay slept on the top of the box till daybreak.

At one place, the party were obliged to cross a river very much flooded by the recent rains. They could not wait for the water to fall, for thunder-storms were coming as frequently as ever. Cross it they must; but how to do it was a most difficult puzzle. This is the way Mackay solved it. One of the carts was stripped of its wheels

PULLING THE CART-BARGE ACROSS THE RIVER

and all other fittings so that when all the cracks were filled with tar, it made a sort of small barge. A few excellent swimmers of the caravan carried a cord across the river. By means of this cord a rope was hauled across and passed around a strong post on the opposite side, and then brought back to the side on which the caravan was stationed. To this pulley the cart-barge was attached. By pulling the rope from one or the other bank, the men carried the barge with its cargo of freight across the river, or brought it back empty to be re-loaded. Other swollen rivers and smaller streams had to be crossed from time to time. It was no mere play to cross any one of them with oxen and carts and baggage which needed to be kept dry.

One day, the accidents were not confined to the carts or baggage, but Mr. Mackay himself was temporarily crippled. He had just succeeded in getting one of the carts over a stream, when he became entangled in a bush and one of the wheels caught his right foot. He fell, and the wheel ran over both his legs. He nearly fainted from the shock; yet a little crude doctoring revived him considerably. Two of his men, putting their loads into the carts, carried him along in a hammock. However, it continued to be a day of troubles; for cart after cart upset. Then too, sick as he was, Mr. Mackay was obliged to turn from patient to doctor; for the chief of a village near by, hearing of his arrival, sent to him seven of his subjects to be vaccinated and one little boy to be cured of spinal disease!

One morning the natives gave Mr. Mackay a unique surprise. Lo, his road had been changed into a field of growing corn. "We thought you white men had cleared this space for us that we might plant gardens," the natives explained.

In reality, they were afraid that the great teams of oxen coming along the white man's road would soon be followed by vast European armies. The farther inland the caravan traveled, the more the natives tried to harass them. In many places, they blocked the road with bushes and trunks of trees; as soon as the cattle were safely across a river, they drove them back to the other side; and became very angry when they saw the oxen tread down the corn planted on the track. Indeed, one chief sent word to Mr. Mackay that if he took his teams past the chief's village he would be shot. Only by patience and skill could headway be made.

Still one more misfortune came upon them, greater than all that have been mentioned. In many parts of the road, the caravan was pestered by the tsetse flies. These were large brownish-yellow insects which, by thousands, stung both the men and the oxen. Although they seemed to bring little more than discomfort to the men, their sting was almost invariably fatal to the animals. When still some distance from Mpwapwa, half of the eighty oxen with which they started were dead, and many more were sick, and it was not many weeks

before the surviving oxen became so few
that the carts were abandoned entirely.

Thus the road had been built at the cost
of nearly one-third of a year's time. With
much difficulty oxen had been trained and
men taught to drive them. Carts had been
brought all the way from India, and much
money had been spent, and months of hard
rough labor had been given to make travel
by carts a success; but the little brown flies
with their poisonous stings spoiled it all.
It was discouraging indeed; but listen to
the missionary, who had done the hardest
work of all.

"Small beginnings may lead to something higher and better in the future, but
the first steps cannot be anything but tedi-
ous. The longest night has always had a
dawn when done, and here I do believe no
far distant time will see a very different
order of things from what has been always
in the past. We are indeed groping in the
dark as to how or what we ought to do first,
but great bodies grow slowly, and the gar-

den of the devil cannot be reclaimed for God all in a year. This will certainly be yet a highway for the King Himself, and all that pass this way will come to know his name.''

Why should this one white man be so hopeful? When traveling on foot, he had barely escaped death from fever. He had failed in building a road. What would he attempt next? Indeed, what was there left for him to try?

CHAPTER IV

TWO RECEPTIONS AT THE ROYAL PALACE

WHAT of the rest of the brave band who started together from England? A grave to be found on a small island off the coast near Zanzibar told the story of one; and by the shores of Victoria Lake on a wooden slab above a mound of earth could have been read the name, "Dr. John Smith." Two more of the party had returned to their English homes as invalids. While Mr. Mackay was still cutting, digging, and leveling for the road to Mpwapwa, the other three members of the party that remained were camping beside the far-reaching waters of Victoria Lake. They were Lieutenant Smith, Mr. O'Neill and Mr. Wilson.

To these men tenting on the lake shore

came two most cordial letters from the king they were so eager to see. Twice canoes appeared before their camps and guides came from Mutesa to escort them to his kingdom. These letters had been written in English by a black boy named Mufta, who had been educated in a Christian school on the coast and had been left by Mr. Stanley with Mutesa to read the Bible to him. This is a copy of the second royal letter:

My Second letter

To My Dear Friend
Wite men

I send this my servant
that you may come quickly
and therefor I pray you.

Come to me quickly and

71

let not this my servant
come without you
And send my Salaam to
Lukonye king of Ukerewe
and Haduma Mwandngwa
of Hageye and Songoro
This from me Mtesa king of Uganda

With so urgent an appeal from the king himself, little wonder is it that two of the white men, leaving Mr. O'Neill to guard their supplies and to repair the steam launch, hastened alone to the northern shore of the lake.

It was about an hour after sunset on a June day in 1877, when their boats were anchored off a little Uganda village at the head of a beautiful bay. Here they were left by their guides who went to the king to announce the coming of the white men. Soon some of Mutesa's chief men arrived to say that they must come to his palace with the escort the king had sent.

A most interesting walk it was to the capital city, taking all of two days. Plantain groves covered thousands of acres of hillsides. Here the missionaries found themselves in a great tropical park, where, through the branches of the trees, glimpses of the beautiful lake could be had. There they wound their way through the thick forest, where the tall trees were heavily festooned with tropical vines of rare beauty. Again, they stopped to rest by a cool, clear stream in the midst of a valley abounding in ferns and palms. On the march once more, they crossed a broad swamp by way of a log road. At last Rubaga, the capital city, was reached, where they were shown to the huts made ready for them by the king's order.

The first day the king paid his respects by sending a rich present of cooking utensils, plantains, potatoes, sugar-cane, milk, *pombe,* venison, and firewood. Promptly

73

at eight o'clock the following morning, two of the chief officers of the king came to escort them to the palace. These officers were superbly costumed in garbs modeled after the Arab style. Their white trousers, tunics, and stockings, were beautifully set off by red shoes and caps. As the missionaries climbed the hill leading to the palace, they were escorted by several soldiers dressed in white, each carrying a flint-lock musket. Behind them paraded a crowd of Waganda dressed for the most part in long, loose brown gowns made from fig-tree bark. Altogether, the officers, the soldiers, the white men, and the crowd in long procession made a sight that was picturesque indeed.

The broad, straight road which led up to the royal hill, superb in itself, was made especially imposing by the tall fence of tiger grass enclosing it on either side. To build these fences posts ten or twelve feet in height were driven into the ground at intervals of a few yards. In and out were then woven long, thick, horizontal ropes of

74

"Officers of the King Came to Escort Them to the Palace"

reed-like grass stalks. Finally to make the meshes closer, there were tied to the fence many vertical stalks of the same kind of grass. Fences such as this lined all the important roads in Uganda and were used also to enclose the private yards about the huts.

At the top of the hill stood Mutesa's palace—a building forty feet in height and supported on each side by straight wooden pillars. The graceful yellow stems of tiger grass formed its walls, and its roof, too, was thatched with grass. With its seventy feet of length, the structure was easily the largest in the realm. To the front of the palace were a number of courts separated from one another by high grass fences, with sliding doors of grass connecting them.

As the white men neared the royal enclosure, a bugle announced their coming, the gates of the courts were opened one by one as the party approached, and quickly closed behind them as they passed. Two lines of white-robed soldiers made a lane through each court, each soldier carrying a gun. As the last gate opened and closed, Lieutenant Smith and Mr. Wilson found themselves before the open door of the palace itself.

In the central hall, on stools ranged in two rows on either side of the entrance, sat all the chiefs of the country. Some were dressed in black, some were in white, and some in red; but all the costumes were of Arabian pattern. All the chiefs arose as the white men entered. The guests were conducted to the upper end of the hall where on a chair of white wood sat his majesty, King Mutesa. The king was wearing a black Arab tunic trimmed with gold braid. His trousers and stockings were white, and his cap and shoes were red. In his belt, he carried a richly mounted sword. At his feet lay a small rug, while the rest of the hall was carpeted with grass.

As the Englishmen approached, Mutesa arose from his throne, shook hands with them, and then by a wave of the hand directed them to two stools near him which had been reserved for them. Forthwith there was much beating of drums. Five minutes of noise gave an opportunity for all in the room to feast their eyes on the central figures of this reception at court. When the drums had finished their din, the king, called one of the messengers whom he had sent to bring the white men to Uganda. He bade him tell the story of their adventures.

Letters were then read from the Sultan of Zanzibar and from the Church Missionary Society in London. The English of the letter from England was translated for the king by Mufta. This was the way it read:

"To His Majesty King Mutesa, Ruler of Uganda.

"Sire:—We have heard with pleasure, through our friend Mr. Stanley, of your earnest invitation to English teachers to come and settle in your kingdom, promising them your favor and protection.

"The greatness of England, of which you have heard, is due to the Word of God which we possess; her laws are framed in accordance with it; her people are made happy by it. Our desire is that your throne should be made secure, your country be made great, and your people made happy by the same means.

"We have resolved, therefore, by the help of God, to send to you two or three of our friends, who will be prepared to settle among your people, and to teach them the Word of God, and other knowledge which will be useful. . . . From what Mr. Stanley has told us, we are sure you will give them a warm welcome when they arrive, and treat them kindly, and take care that they want nothing.

"Commending you to the grace and blessing of the Most High God, who is King of kings and Lord of lords, and whose servants we are,

We desire to subscribe ourselves,
Your Majesty's friends and well-wishers."

In the midst of the reading of the letter, the king ordered the firing of a salute, and

78

a general rejoicing to be made, and at the close of the reading, the expressions of gladness seemed to have no bounds. The king, half rising from his chair, called his chief musician and ordered a more vigorous rejoicing. Drums were beaten, horns were blown, and all the assembly of chiefs were bowing their heads and clapping their hands, and saying again and again, *"Nyanzig," "Nyanzig,"* "We thank you," "We thank you." The king asked his interpreter to tell the white men that what they saw and heard was all for the name of Jesus.

After some conversation, the white men presented their gifts to the king. These included a Turkish rug, a map of Africa, photographs, and other articles. Lieutenant Smith apologized for the small number of things they had to give, saying that some had been stolen from them on the way.

To this the king graciously replied: "Great rivers swallow up small ones. Now I have seen your faces, I do not look on the presents."

The next morning the missionaries had a second conversation with the king in the presence of all his chiefs and courtiers. For some reason, Mutesa seemed suspicious of them and began to inquire about General Gordon of the English army in Egypt. He wanted the white men to make guns and gunpowder, at the same time confessing "My heart is not good." The missionaries told him that they had to do as the letter said and not to make guns; and that if he did not wish them to stay, they would leave Uganda. For some time he was silent, then asked: "What have you come for—to teach my people to read and write?"

"Yes," they replied, "and whatever useful arts we and those coming may know."

Then calling his interpreter, the king said: "Tell them now my heart is good; England is my friend. I have one hand in Uganda, and the other in England."

When the missionaries reached their huts after the morning *baraza* [court] was over, there came to them a messenger from Mutesa saying that there was one more word which he wanted to say to them, but he had been afraid to say it before all the people. Eager to know what this further message was, Lieutenant Smith and Mr. Wilson in the afternoon went a third time to the king's palace. They found him seated in a side room with only a few chiefs and one wife present.

He said: "There is one word I want to say to you. I was afraid to speak it this morning because the Arabs were present. This is it,—Did you bring 'The Book'? That is all I want."

They told him they had it in English and Arabic, and part of it in the language spoken at the coast which Mutesa knew slightly, and they hoped soon to give it to him in Luganda [the language of Uganda].

Then Mutesa's heart was very good. He took the white men out into his palace grounds and showed them the beautiful views which could be had from various positions. He also pointed out two sites which he said he would give them, one for a mission house, the other for a school.

"When will they be built?" they asked.

"To-morrow my people shall go and bring wood," and the king was as good as his word; for the next day the work began.

Such a welcome was most encouraging. After a month's stay in the hut Mutesa had built for them, Lieutenant Smith said good-by to Mr. Wilson and started for the southern end of the lake to tell Mr. O'Neill how royally Mutesa had received them. He expected to help Mr. O'Neill launch the missionary boat and pack supplies. Then together they would return to Uganda. But their hopes were never realized. While on one of the islands in the southern part of the lake, both Mr. Smith and Mr. O'Neill were heartlessly murdered by the natives.

The terrible news was reported to Mr. Mackay before his oxen and carts had reached Mpwapwa. His cattle had been dying three and four a day. The dusky natives were daily jeering at the white man's failure. He himself had just recovered from another attack of fever. Just at that moment, he heard that two more of their band had been taken from them.

Broken-hearted, yet believing in his God, he wrote to a friend at home: "Our good doctor, my own dear friend of many years, went to his rest nine months ago, and now these brave brothers, Smith and O'Neill, have fallen. There were eight of us sent out—two invalided and four gone home! Only two remaining. Poor Africa! When will it become a Christian country at this rate? But God has other hands in reserve, whom he will bring to the front, fast and unexpectedly, and the work will go on whether we break down or not."

Since a wealthy Arab merchant had been murdered along with the missionaries, Mr. Mackay was afraid that the Arabs would take revenge on the king who had murdered them. Eager to prevent further bloodshed, he decided to hurry to the lake as fast as possible.

Bundles and bags were safely stored, and Mr. Tytherleigh was left to see that the best two of the carts, emptied of all freight, were dragged to Mpwapwa. Mackay himself sped forward as fast as possible. Five days of quick marching, wading and swimming through jungles, swamps, and rivers, brought him to Mpwapwa. A brief rest, and he was again on a forced march, with only six men to carry outfit, food, and medicine.

Although hurrying as fast as he was able, he saw three months go by before he reached Kagei, a little town on the southern shore of Victoria Lake. The body of his only white companion, Mr. Tytherleigh, was laid in a grave by the way. Mr. Mackay tramped through jungles, plodded along sandy deserts, and picked his way over stony stretches till his feet were blistered and bleeding. Every step was painful. Repeated attacks of fever reduced him almost to a skeleton. But on the evening of the thirteenth of June, forgetting his weakness and pain, with intense joy he stood on the shore of Victoria

Lake. At last his miserable marching was over, and he too could hope soon to present himself at the court of King Mutesa.

June passed, and July, and August. Indeed it was not till November (1878), that Mr. Mackay entered the capital of Uganda. Two years and a half had passed since he had said good-by to his friends in the homeland. Two years and a half spent merely in traveling! And he had not yet even seen the king who had asked Stanley to send him missionaries.

But Mutesa had not forgotten his request. For over a year Mr. Wilson had lived near his palace, and the black king had learned to like him. Mr. Wilson had told his Majesty of the other white man who was on his way, and Mutesa grew very eager to receive Mr. Mackay. But the day he arrived the king was ill. He merely sent his salaams and two fat goats. Two days later, however, word came that the king was holding *baraza,* and wished to see Mr. Wilson and Mr. Mackay at once. Carrying their presents

85

with them they started off for the palace. Mr. Mackay will tell his own story of their reception.

"Messenger after messenger came running like madmen to hurry us on, but I was determined not to give way to the frantic behavior of these excited couriers, and kept a steady step. At length we entered on the grand esplanade, running east and west along the top of the hill and ending in the palace at the west end. The gates were opened, the grand guard presented arms, and we passed along through the double row of guards, into a large hall, densely lined with courtiers. At the far end was a door, through which we were ushered into the presence of the king. Here he was, seated on a mat, dressed in a long white robe and long black coat richly embroidered with gold braid. He bowed politely, and stools were brought for us to sit on, while some Turkish-dressed attendants squatted on the ground. An old woman sat behind the king, a little way off, and watched intently. For ten

86

minutes we eyed each other in dead silence. Then a little talk began. Our gifts were presented, and the music-box struck up the fine air, 'The heavens are telling,' from Haydn's oratorio called 'Creation.'

"We talked with him on many subjects for an hour. The king told us he had been led to suspect the coming of Englishmen to his country as a danger to his throne, but now a year had passed since Lieutenant Smith and Mr. Wilson first arrived, and all his intercourse with our party had only tended to raise us in his favor.

"After some time the king intimated that he was too ill to sit long, and gave us permission to go. We left, the whole court rising and following us down the hill—small boys, as usual, forming a majority of the spectators and followers. In the evening the king sent us no less than ten fat cattle as a present, and a man's load of tobacco with a like quantity of both coffee and honey."

This then was the sort of reception given by King Mutesa to the first English missionaries of Uganda. He showed every sign of being glad to have them in his country. He supplied them generously with food. He gave them huts to live in. He built them a mission house and school building. At court he listened attentively to their messages. He observed the Christian Sabbath, and welcomed Christian services at his court. Every prospect was encouraging, and with gratitude the missionaries carried on their work.

CHAPTER V

WHITE MEN AND BLACK MEN BECOME ACQUAINTED

A MILE and a half down the hill from Mutesa's palace was the grass hut where lived the two white men. During the first few weeks after their arrival, they had lived nearer the royal hill; but, because of the jealousy of the chiefs, the king was obliged to have their quarters moved farther away, for according to custom the greatest chief should live nearest the palace. The Arabs, too, were jealous and had told the king that if he allowed the white men to build their own home, it would be a fortress of brick, and they would soon take his kingdom away from him.

So the white men's African home was nothing but a rectangular hut with open spaces left in the tiger-grass walls for windows. The thatched roof was shaped something like a cocked hat; and in front, it extended a few feet beyond the walls, making a sort of veranda. The rooms within, formed by tiger-grass partitions, were broken up by numerous poles which served as roof-supports, and in the dark as obstacles to bump against.

Mutesa had given the white men almost two acres of land, and it was not long before a number of houses were built upon it. Within four months after Mr. Mackay's arrival, five missionary recruits from England reached the capital, making in all a party of seven missionaries. As homes for these several other huts were built. One man being a doctor, built a dispensary where he might receive his patients. Mr. Mackay put up two workshops where he might have a school of mechanics. A schoolhouse was king Mutesa's gift. An extensive garden was planted with vegetable seeds brought from England. Five hundred banana plants

90

were set out, and the entire plot of land enclosed by a tall tiger-grass fence. Before long, the missionary headquarters began to be very attractive.

It is true that in such primitive dwellings not a few discomforts had to be undergone. Had the missionaries enjoyed anything better than a mud floor or indulged in more than a few pieces of plain furniture, the natives would have become suspicious. Yet the white men were ambitious to show themselves true friends of the black men, and so every day it was their custom to eat some plain native foods. Frequently they would sit down in the home of a friendly native of Uganda to a meal of meat and bananas. But, try as hard as they might to live plainly among the natives, there were many things about them and their actions which seemed strange to the black men.

The large oval table was a most wonderful piece of furniture to the Waganda. To us it would have seemed a very crude affair, for Mr. Mackay had made it by screwing to-

gether two big half-oval parts of the steam
launch, and mounting them on six poles
which were stuck in the mud floor. Then
too the black men were bewildered by the
strange fire [the lamp] which the white men
kept burning on the table from which they
ate. The knives and forks also perplexed
the natives, who were accustomed to use
only their fingers for handling food. "Perhaps," they thought, "these long, stiff
things the white men eat with are a part of
their hands." They looked with curious
eyes on the white men's clothes; their
shoes, especially, were beyond comprehen-
sion. "Why is it," they asked themselves,
"that the Englishmen have white faces and
hands and black feet with toes all joined
into one?"

All these and other odd customs made the
Waganda flock in crowds to stare at the
strangers and to watch the things they did.
But after a few months had passed, the
novelty began to wear off, and the missionaries were no longer feared. The chiefs be-

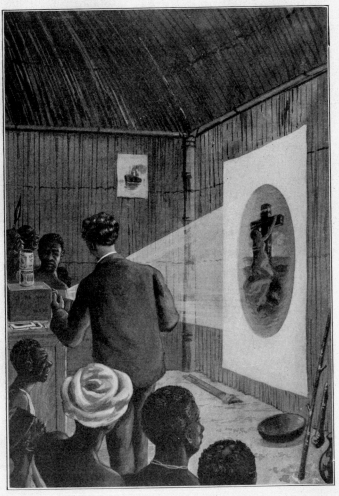

" The Marvels of the Magic Lantern "

came their friends, and every day one or more of them called.

The white men continued to do many things which seemed most wonderful to the ignorant people of Uganda. From the first, Mackay became a special favorite of the king and chiefs because of the marvelous things he could make. Often Mr. Mackay's workshop was filled with chiefs and slaves together, who stood and gazed with curiosity as he toiled away with his tools. His blacksmith's forge and bellows and his turning-lathe were marvels unseen before in Uganda; and, as they saw him sharpen a knife on the revolving grindstone, they were greatly puzzled to know what made the wheels go round.

In the evenings Mr. Mackay often delighted a company of natives with the marvels of the magic lantern. What mattered it to them that the chimney had been built of two biscuit cans, one placed on top of the other and tacked into a wooden box? Their wonder centered in the pictures.

When Mr. Mackay's skill became widely known, miscellaneous articles for him to repair were heaped upon the bench in his workshop. Native-made steel hoes and hatchets were given him to temper. They said it was by means of witchcraft that he was able to put hardness into steel and then take it out again. No kind of wheel had ever before been seen in Uganda, and any sort of rotary motion seemed marvelous to the natives. Even when one day he rolled several logs up a hill, great crowds followed him, crying, *"Makay lubare! Makay lubare dala!"* ["Mackay is the great spirit; Mackay is truly the great spirit."]

On one occasion, Mutesa asked to see a steam-engine. Mr. Mackay tells the story: "I went up with one from the steam launch we brought last trip—the first article of the kind ever in this part of the world. The king asked many intelligent questions about it. I took a screw-key with me to show how the parts can be taken asunder, when the king came out with one of his 'pretty sayings.' He said, 'White men's wisdom comes from God. They see the human body is all in pieces—joints and limbs—and that is why they make such things in pieces too!'"

"After much talk, he asked how white men came to know so much—did they always know these things? I replied that once Englishmen were savages and knew nothing at all, but from the day we became Christians our knowledge grew more and more, and every year we were wiser than we were before."

"I guess God will not prosper any man," the king said, "that does not please him."

"God is kind to all," Mackay answered, "but especially to these who love and fear him."

"*Eh, Eh*" ["Yes, Yes"] answered Mutesa.

So, because of his mechanical skill, Mr. Mackay had an opportunity to teach Mutesa and his court who the people are who really prosper and become wise.

However, it did not satisfy Mr. Mackay

to have the crowds look up to him as the
great man who was able to make anything.
His ambition was to gather pupils and to
teach them to make useful things for their
own people.

At first Mutesa would not allow any one
to be taught, neither did the men and boys
wish to learn, for in Uganda it was an honor
for a man to be idle. In that tropical climate and rich country, little or no work
needed to be done to obtain abundant crops
of fruits and vegetables. To support a
large family with their simple ways of living meant little labor for the head of the
house. What work was to be done was
given to the slaves and the women. A
"gentleman" in Uganda, therefore, had little to do but to order his slaves and wives
about, and to attend the daily *baraza* of the
king. That Mr. Mackay was willing to
work with his hands was not the least wonderful thing about him. It required a long
time for him to teach them that a Christian
ought not to be an idle man.

96

It was not so difficult a task to persuade the natives to come to the missionaries' house to learn to read. At first the king forbade any going to the white men even for this purpose, probably because he was afraid they would soon be able to outstrip him in their ability to read.

It was little more than a month, however, after Mackay's arrival when the edict was withdrawn, and Mr. Mackay wrote: "I have a whole lot of pupils, old and young. Some have made wonderful progress already, for Waganda are most apt, as a rule. I find the slaves, however, usually twice as quick as their masters."

It was the English alphabet which he taught them, but Luganda words which they learned to spell. On large sheets of paper the missionaries copied big, clear letters, making easy syllables or words and sentences. The number of pupils steadily increased, so that it was difficult for the missionaries to make reading sheets fast enough.

97

The coming of these pupils, eager to learn to read, was most encouraging; yet the missionaries' opportunities for being helpful to the Waganda were not confined to their homes and the schoolhouse. King Mutesa was urgent in his frequent invitations to them to attend the morning *baraza* at the palace, and to tell him and his chiefs of the ways of white men and their religion. Every Sabbath morning it was his custom to hold a religious service in the palace. At these times, week days and Sundays, the missionaries talked on many subjects to the king and his chiefs. Sometimes it was about the two countries, England and Uganda.

"You would sometimes be amused to hear the high idea entertained by the king and people about their own country," Mr. Mackay wrote, "It is only natural, however. Not long ago Mutesa said to me: 'Mackay, when I become friends with England, God in heaven will be witness that England will not come to make war on Uganda, nor

Uganda go to make war on England! And when I go to England,' he continued, 'I shall take greatness and glory with me, and shall bring greatness and glory back again. Every one will say, 'Oh, Mutesa is coming!' when I reach England; and when I return, 'Oh, Mutesa is coming back again!' "

"Of course, at such statements I only look very grave, and say, 'Just so, exactly.' At present, (do not laugh) Mutesa really believes that Uganda is the most powerful country in the world. Though he fears Egypt, he has often spoken of going to fight against Colonel Gordon. I have had some stiff arguments with him on this point. You will understand that in such matters I must be very careful. A king that is used to nothing but flattery from his courtiers, whose lives he can take at any moment if they do anything other than flatter him, is no ordinary individual to speak plainly to. One needs a smooth tongue when speaking to him.

"I do not mean to say that I am afraid of

him, but there is no use giving offense. And yet the truth can be told, although not in just so many words. In sacred matters, however, I do very differently. In teaching the relations between man and God I make no mincing of matters. When I have to say what goes hard against heathen custom and pride and love of self, I give my message, saying it is not mine but God's command.''

King Mutesa was quick to understand what was explained to him; yet things which are very commonplace to civilized men he had never heard of before. When Mr. Mackay told him in a simple way about the railroads and steamships, and explained what the telephone and telegraph could do, the king was greatly delighted.

This is the way Mackay summed it up, and Mutesa was deeply impressed: ''My forefathers made the wind their slave; then they enchained water; next they enslaved steam; but now the terrible lightning is the white man's slave, and a capital one it is, too!''

100

Their first Christmas in Uganda was duly celebrated at court. Mr. Mackay having explained the meaning of the day, a great flag was hoisted above the palace, as was usual on Sundays, and all the chiefs appeared in extraordinary dress. Mr. Mackay read the story of the birth of Jesus, as told in St. Luke's Gospel, and explained the meaning of the song of the angels. Being asked to tell more, he related the story of Jesus' boyhood and young manhood at Nazareth, and tried to show by Jesus' example, that it was an honor to work with one's hands.

Some days later, an Arab trader presented himself at court with guns and cloth which he wanted to sell for slaves. He offered one red cloth for one slave; one musket for two slaves; and one hundred percussion caps for one female slave.

Since Mackay was present that morning, he was given an opportunity to speak. In the presence of all the chiefs and courtiers, he told the king how cruelly the poor slaves were treated during their journeys to the

101

coast. Mutesa was so much moved that he declared he would sell no more slaves to the Arabs, and the traders were obliged to sell their guns and cloth for ivory only.

Some days later, Mr. Mackay took a book on physiology to the palace. By means of pictures, he showed the king the different parts of the body, and how the blood circulates through them all. He explained many things so that Mutesa might see how wonderfully perfect the human body is, and that no man or group of men in all the world could ever make one. "Yet," he said, "the Arabs wish to buy these perfect bodies with immortal souls within them, each for a rag of cloth which one man can make in a day."

Mutesa was convinced of the wrong, and decreed that from that time no one in his kingdom should sell a slave on pain of death.

"The best decree you have ever made, King Mutesa," said Mr. Mackay: but alas, it was one thing for Mutesa to make a decree and another to see that his words were faithfully carried out.

Often on Sabbaths Mr. Mackay read to the king some of the parables Jesus told. One day, he read the story of the old garment and the new cloth (Luke v. 36), how it was not wise to tear a piece off of a new garment and patch an old garment with it; for the new garment would be spoiled and the patch would not look well on the old gown.

So, he told the king, it was just as foolish for him to patch up his old heathen life by doing a few Christian things. It was no use for him to try to be a heathen and a Christian at the same time, to keep on living with his three hundred wives and to pretend to be a Christian; to buy and sell God's children as slaves, and to claim to follow Jesus; to treat his subjects cruelly and to order them killed for every little offense, and still to pray at Christian service on Sunday.

Another morning at court, Mr. Mackay read the parable of the sower and the seed, and invited the king and chiefs to talk freely

103

together about it. Mutesa was so deeply impressed by the explanation of the parable that he said to his chiefs, *"Isa* [Jesus], was there ever any one like him?"

So at the beginning of their life in Uganda there was much to encourage the missionaries. But King Mutesa was not always the earnest, interested learner he seemed at first to be. He was a king with two very different faces, and he showed whichever he chose when the white men were present.

Shortly after Mr. Mackay arrived in Uganda, the missionaries were surprised to learn that a group of French Catholic priests were on their way to Mutesa's land. On their arrival, the king received them with his accustomed cordiality and pomp. But from that time trouble began. Protestants and Catholics both believe themselves to be Christians, yet their beliefs about Christ and the Bible are not alike.

King Mutesa seemed bewildered. "Every white man has a different religion," he said. "What am I to believe? Who is right?

First I was a heathen, then a Mohammedan, then a Christian; now other white men come and tell me these English are wrong. Perhaps if I follow these new men, then other white men will come and tell me these also are wrong." Sometimes King Mutesa was kind to the French missionaries: sometimes he seemed to favor the English more. Sometimes he was disagreeable to both. Since the white men in the country were regarded as the personal guests of the king, Mutesa was expected to give them homes to live in and from his royal bounty to provide their daily food. This he did most generously until after the French Catholics came. Then many a day both English and French alike suffered from hunger because Mutesa neglected to send them bananas and cowry-shells, which were Uganda money. The urgent suggestion even reached the Englishmen that they should "clear out as quickly as possible, as the king's soldiers were only waiting to kill them all." Later by several weeks, they heard that Mutesa was very ill and did not expect to recover; that a meeting of chiefs and Arabs had been held, at which it was decided to murder all the Englishmen, should Mutesa die.

Requests from the missionaries for permission to leave the country were persistently refused by the king. Finally, however, he decided to send three of his own subjects to visit the great Queen Victoria and two missionaries were allowed to go as an escort. Two others of the party left Uganda to start missionary work in a city several hundred miles south of the end of the lake, and Mr. Pearson accompanied them for a short distance, to get supplies. For some months, Mr. Mackay and Mr. Litchfield were left alone in Uganda.

Strange to say, during these months King Mutesa turned about and showed his better face. In the many discussions at court from week to week, he usually took Mackay's part. The Sunday services again were held regularly.

106

Mutesa became enthusiastic over the subject of book knowledge, and even commanded all his chiefs, officials, pages, and soldiers to learn to read. No one could quite explain the sudden change which had come over him. The mission house was besieged by eager learners. All day long Mackay and Litchfield were never without pupils about them, some of whom were waiting even at daylight. It was fortunate for them that the small printing-press had arrived. Long into the night they worked, printing sheets which during the day men and boys were taught to read. All the blank paper they had was used and much of their personal writing-paper; yet the demand could not be satisfied.

On his return from the southern end of the lake, Mr. Pearson was greatly surprised at the change in the situation. "On several occasions, when going to the palace," said he, "I saw small groups sitting under the shade of some high fence, going through their sheets; on the way I met many carrying their sheets rolled up nicely, with a covering of bark cloth for the hand. At the court the chiefs sat waiting for the king to open *baraza,* and passed the time with their sheets.

"I had one thought in my mind, surely this is the finger of God."

King Mutesa would have done for a Chinese puzzle. One Sabbath in court, in the midst of the enthusiasm over reading, he made a sudden request of Mr. Mackay. After the Scripture lesson was read, he asked abruptly, "Can any one baptize?"

"No," was the answer.

"Can you?"

"No, but the clergyman is qualified to do so."

"I wish to be baptized and my chiefs."

Mr. Mackay told the king that only those who were true Christians should be baptized. Jesus had said, as one could tell the kind of tree by the fruit it bore, so one could tell a true Christian by the sort of life he lived. Mr. Mackay had not seen either him or his chiefs giving up lying, witchcraft, murder, Sabbath-breaking, or any of their evil habits. Then, too, if the king wished to be baptized, he must be willing to live with only one wife.

Mutesa acknowledged that the Uganda custom of having a great many wives did much harm; yet he had once resolved to live two years with no wife at all, he said, but after two months he did as he had always done.

Several days later, Mackay went to the palace and found the king arguing with the Arabs over the Koran, their sacred book. He again showed interest in the subject of baptism. He said he would put away his wives and follow Christ truly. He wanted one wife only in their place, and preferred that she be a white woman. Since he was a king, he said, his wife should be a king's daughter. He tried to persuade Mr. Mackay to write to Queen Victoria for one of her daughters. He would give a thousand elephant tusks for her.

Mr. Mackay told him that he would probably not be able to get her, for in England no woman ever married unless she wished to do so. At this, Mutesa was very much surprised, and without more ado court was dismissed.

Like the tall grass about his own courtyard when shaken by the wind, Mutesa swayed back and forth, uncertain in his attitude towards his visitors. He gloried over having the white men in his capital because of the presents they brought and the things they could do. Now he would favor the French, and again he would favor the English, so that he could keep them both in the country. The missionaries knew not what to expect of him or how much to believe of what he said. Yet there was no insult or privation they were unwilling to endure if only in the end Mutesa could be brought to be a follower of Christ.

CHAPTER VI

THE KING AND THE WIZARD

ABOUT Christmas time in the year 1879, there were two names which, in the region of Uganda's capital, seemed to be on everybody's lips. One was that of Mukasa, the great wizard who lived on an island in Victoria Lake, and the other was the name of Mr. Mackay. The great wizard's name was always spoken with reverence and fear; Mackay's was usually coupled with a curse. Indeed, many would have been glad to see him tortured to death.

For some time it had been rumored that the great wizard of the lake was on his way to the capital. Month after month, Arab traders had tried to get away from the country to take their ivory and slaves to the coast; but, when they went to the port on the lake, they were always refused canoes because, it was said, "The great wizard of the Lake is about to visit the king." The great spirit or god of Uganda was supposed to be living within this wizard, and for this reason he was greatly feared.

Many other less powerful spirits or gods were worshiped by the Waganda. When the people were anxious about their crops, they went to the god of food; when threatened by famine, they went to the god of famine; in time of war offerings were made to the god of war; on other occasions, it was the god of the earthquake, or the god of the plague, or the god of the smallpox, which was most worshiped.

Here and there, along the roadside, under some tree, or in the private courtyards of the chiefs were to be seen the tiny huts, already described, which were sacred to one or another of these gods. In some of them dwelt the wizards and witches, in whom the spirits or gods were supposed to live.

Very plainly were these strange folk

"The Great Wizard of the Lake is About to Visit the King"

dressed, usually in simple robes of goat-skins only; and they carried clubs of crooked wood decorated with iron knobs and bells. Now and then a wizard, assuming a high falsetto voice, would rave like a lunatic. The people thinking that the spirit within him was angry, would bring him cows and chickens and goats as gifts and even a great many pots of beer, for the spirits were supposed to need very much to drink. When offering such gifts the Waganda would be praying the best kind of prayers they knew, while the wizard would make them think more prayers were needed.

These men and women of magic also made a great many trinkets, sometimes simply from bunches of grass, or again from the teeth of animals, or from odd-shaped stones. After mumbling mysterious words over these trifles, the sacred men sold the trinkets to the people as charms. When worn about the neck or ankles, or when placed above the doorways of the homes or hung about the tiny huts where they made their offerings, the Waganda thought these charms a protection against the numerous evils over which the gods had control.

Of all these spirits, the greatest was the god of the lake. If a chief wished to learn what this god could tell him of the chances for success in some war, shortly to be entered upon, he would go to the god's island home in the lake. There lived an old man, named Mukasa, the god's wizard.

The chief would meet the wizard in a small, dark hut, where there was a little wooden stool covered with a heap of bark cloth. On one end of the leopard skin on which stood the sacred stool, the chief would kneel, and on the other end the old wizard would take his place. After some time the spirit would supposedly enter underneath the bark cloths over the stool. The wizard, thereupon, would be thrown into a frenzy and would pour forth unearthly noises, giving the chief now and then a word which might be understood. After being duly impressed by this weird proceeding, the chief

114

would leave, believing that he had heard the words of the great spirit.

Mukasa, the great wizard of the lake, now actually left his island home and visited the capital of Uganda. For two years king Mutesa had suffered with a painful disease. Many native doctors had tried to cure him. For a time he had been treated by one of the missionaries, who was a physician, and Mutesa was temporarily benefited; but refusing to give up some of his wicked habits of life which had first brought on the trouble, he received no permanent good. Since he suffered intensely and was daily growing weaker, it was rumored again and again that he would soon die.

Finally, the queen mother together with his wives urged him to go to Mukasa, the wizard of the great spirit, who they were confident could heal him. Upon his insisting that he could not leave the capital, they persuaded him to allow Mukasa to come to him.

At last the wizard came, and his camp was

set up a mile and a half southwest of the missionaries' headquarters. Every day could be heard the roll of drums beaten in his honor, and men carrying dozens of loads of plantains from the king to the wizard's camp passed by the missionaries' house. Cattle, chickens, and even servants were sent as presents to him. He would heal the king by a single word, every one was saying. It would be some days, however, before he would make his way to the palace; for he must wait for the coming of the new moon to begin his work.

These days of waiting seemed to the missionaries most critical days. Should king Mutesa receive this heathen wizard at his court, he would be announcing to all his subjects that he had wholly rejected the white man's religion and was again as much a heathen as ever in the past. To think that perhaps their two years' work would end in such a failure, was sorely disappointing. If ever they prayed earnestly they did now. Every opportunity that arose, they were determined to use in trying to persuade King Mutesa to refuse to see this heathen sorcerer.

The morning of Thursday, December the eleventh, brought a day long remembered among the court folk and the missionaries. *Baraza* had already commenced when Mr. Mackay arrived. After various subjects had been discussed, and seeing that Mutesa was in good spirits, Mr. Mackay stepped forward and sat down on a stool before the king.

"May I have permission to ask one question of the king?" he said.

Mutesa replied, "Say on."

"What is a wizard?" he asked.

The question was a surprise to every one. Some were offended, because they believed in the power of the wizard; others smiled, because they thought that the people were believing foolishness. Mutesa seemed to take the question kindly, and began to explain what wizards were, that in them lived the spirits of the gods. He also said that the

117

remains of his dead ancestors were guarded by persons who were believed to be able to talk with the departed spirits, and that at times the spirits of the dead kings entered into them.

Mr. Mackay told him that there were no living men who could talk with the spirits of the dead and that those who claimed they could do so told falsehoods, that there were many men of that sort in Uganda, but the chief of them all was the wizard Mukasa.

"I believe you have little confidence in the powers of such pretenders," he continued, "but I have heard that several of your chiefs have been advising you to go to the wizard to be cured. I sit before you, your servant and the servant of Almighty God, and in his name I beg of you have no dealings with this wizard, whether a chief tries to persuade you to do so, or a common man advises you." The king did not seem to oppose him, and translated his words to the court.

Mr. Mackay continued: "If this Mukasa

is a wizard, then he is a god, and thus there are two gods in Uganda—the Lord God Almighty and Mukasa; but if Mukasa is only a man, as many say he is, then there are two kings in Uganda—Mutesa, whom we all acknowledge and honor, and this Mukasa, who gives himself out as some great one.''

Mutesa seemed to see the point and again translated Mackay's words to the court. He told him that he was intending to hold a council of his chiefs with a view to coming to some decision in the matter. Mr. Mackay urged that there was no need of that; for, if the king himself believed the wizard to be an enemy of God, it would not be difficult for him to lead his chiefs to see how absurd the wizard's claims were.

Then Mutesa opened a discussion with his chiefs on ''What is a wizard?'' He ended the talk by saying, ''If the wizard is a man, he is not a wizard; for a wizard is a spirit or god.''

One of Mr. Mackay's letters gives the rest of the story of that day at court: ''I said

119

that this Mukasa was practically causing rebellion in the country, for he disobeyed Mutesa's orders, and asserted his right over the
Lake as before that of the king. It was
more than five months since Mutesa had ordered his Arab traders to be supplied with
boats to go to Usukuma, [district of Kagei]
yet those traders were not able to start because of Mukasa's counter-orders. This
was a state of things that should not be allowed to exist. In the Book of God I was
prepared to show him that both in the Old
and New Testaments all sorcerers were de-
nounced as liars, and were ranked in the
lowest scale of iniquity. Moses commanded
them to be put to death. In our own country, in times past, they were put to the stake.
But we did not as Christians sanction so severe a measure, nor did we come here to advise the shedding of blood; but still, on looking at the express command of God as stated
in his Book, we did advise that every man
who deceived people into believing that he
was possessed of a spirit should be ordered

120

to cease such deception, and if he chose to continue it, he should be sent to prison. These men were great liars, and Mukasa, as the head wizard, was the greatest liar, and the greatest rebel in the country.

"Mutesa seemed rather delighted at the decidedness with which I spoke, and translated everything, even recurring to the other way I put it: 'If Mukasa is a god, we have two gods; if he is a man, then there are two kings here.' Those who were at first inclined to defend the evil genius had at length nothing to say for him. Mutesa's prime minister mentioned that Lukonge called himself god of the south end of the lake. One of the Arabs recommended waiting a couple of days to see what Mukasa had to say for himself. 'What was to be done?' was the question."

" 'Lukonge is a heathen,' I said, 'and knows not God.'

" 'But I know God,' Mutesa responded.

"Yes, it is because you know God, and I believe wish to serve him, that I now ask

121

you to choose one or the other, and not to honor an enemy of God. In all history we read that God was with every king that feared him, while those who went astray after other gods came to an end of shame. God has said, 'Them that honor me I will honor; and they that despise me shall be lightly esteemed.'"

Some loads of plantains and other donations were at this moment presented, and other disturbances arising, Mutesa told Mackay that the subject would have to be dropped for the time, but he would attend to what Mackay had said. Thanking the king, the white man retired to his seat.

When court was dismissed, the missionary received many a friendly hand-shake from the chiefs. Some of them, who, he supposed, were the strongest advocates of the wizard, greeted him in a friendly way, although some of them gave him the curious look of those who felt they had been defeated.

Another opportunity came the next Sabbath. "The day was very fine," Mr. Mackay wrote, "and many were present at service. After prayers, instead of our usual reading in St. Luke, I turned over the Scriptures from Exodus to Revelation, reading a host of passages to show the mind of God toward dealers in witchcraft. The laws of God to Moses, the examples of Saul and of Ahaziah, the manifestation of our Lord to destroy the works of the devil, the Acts of the Apostles—especially the case of Elymas—the works of the flesh contrasted with the fruit of the Spirit in Galatians, fifth chapter, and, finally, the list of those who may not enter through the gates of the heavenly city (Revelation xxii. 15). All these I read, in order, having previously written out the passages.

"I had wonderful attention to-day—much more than usual. I was gratified to hear one of the chiefs say that the list of passages read was enough to set the matter at rest, and there could be no more dispute as to the unlawfulness of witchcraft."

123

It was but a few nights till the new moon would appear. The following Saturday, however, brought disappointing news. Mr. Mackay heard from one of his pupils that all the chiefs had supplied men to build three small huts for Mukasa and his companions in the king's inner court, and that they had worked late by moonlight in order to have them finished by Monday morning when the wizard was to arrive.

There was still a little more delay, however, and Mukasa did not arrive as soon as was expected. Mackay was given another opportunity to speak to the king Monday morning. A few minutes after all were seated for the *baraza,* Mr. Mackay arose and sat down in front of the king, squatting like a tailor on the floor, as all the chiefs and Arabs did.

Mutesa seemed to know what Mackay wanted to talk about, and he gave orders for all music and other noises outside the court to cease at once.

"Is it your pleasure, King Mutesa,"

124

Mackay began, "that I should cease teaching the Word of God at court on Sundays?"

"No, not by any means."

"You and your chiefs," continued Mackay, "have now made up your minds to bring the wizard to stay at court. The other day your majesty admitted that he was a deceiver. I have no right to interfere with your orders or whom you choose as your guest; only this visitor, for whom preparations are made, is no ordinary guest, but is looked up to by the people as possessed of powers which belong to God alone; We cannot mix up the worship of God Almighty with the worship of a man who is the enemy of God."

Mutesa listened intently, and then said to his chiefs, "Do you hear what Mackay says? He says that we cannot bring the wizard here without offending God."

"The wizard is only coming with medicine to heal the king," one of the chiefs answered.

Mackay replied, "The wizard is not

125

merely a doctor, but is looked up to by all as a god, and as being able to heal people by enchantment."

"The white man is right," admitted the king. "I know very well that this Mukasa is coming to use witchcraft."

"We should only be delighted if Mukasa could cure the king," continued Mackay, "and neither I nor any other missionary would object to his bringing medicine for that purpose."

"Gabunga [the head chief on the lake] came some time ago to say that Mukasa was able to cure me," said the king. " 'Bring his medicine, then,' I said. Gabunga brought some; but said it was of no use unless the wizard were present himself to perform the cure. This and that other fellow says that he is a wizard and that the spirit of my ancestors has gone into him; but do you think I believe that?"

"I believe Mutesa has more sense than to believe anything of the kind," said Mackay, "for when a man dies, his soul returns to

126

God, so that these fellows are only liars, and deceive the people.''

The king replied, "What you say, Mackay, is perfectly true, and I know that all witchcraft is falsehood.''

Mackay thanked Mutesa for this statement, but the prime minister and other chiefs did not seem pleased. They saw no harm in the wizard being received with all honor. He would make medicine which they would hang up in the palace-houses, as Mukasa was a great medicine-man.

"Medicine is an excellent thing,'' repeated Mackay, "but it is not medicine that has given Mukasa so great a name. This is not the reason why he is regarded as a wizard, but he wishes the people to believe him a god.''

Again the king seemed to agree with all Mr. Mackay had said. Much discussion followed. Sometimes the chiefs seemed to side with the white man, but usually they were opposed to him. Again Mackay pleaded with Mutesa, saying:

127

"I cannot hinder the king from having the wizard as many days at court as he likes, only I find it my duty to tell him that his encouraging this false person will have a powerful effect in the country in making the people believe more strongly than ever in witches and wizards, while King Mutesa himself does not believe in them. I take my stand on the Word of God, which says that all who use witchcraft are enemies of God."

Poor Mutesa knew not what to do. His mother and his friends had persuaded him to have the wizard brought to his capital. He acknowledged that it would be wrong to receive him; yet he was afraid not to do as his mother and his chiefs wished.

"We are all ready to honor and respect your mother and your relatives," again Mackay urged, "but God is greater than them all, and you must choose which you will serve, God, or your relatives." *Baraza* was soon dismissed.

Mackay's last opportunity to plead at

court came two days before Christmas. When all were seated, Mr. Mackay was called forward, and a woman was brought in.

Mutesa said to Mackay, "This woman, my aunt, has been sent to bring you to the council of my mother, and others of the family, that you may explain to them why you refuse to allow me to see the wizard."

"I will not go to explain at any other court than this," Mackay replied. "I do not refuse to allow your majesty to see the wizard: only as a servant of God I warn you of the sin of witchcraft. I use no force, but, as I told your majesty yesterday, it was my place to tell you the truth, while you are free to follow or reject my advice."

All the chiefs began to talk at once, and the king grew afraid not to act as they wished.

Mutesa then said, "Now we will leave both the Arab's religion and the *Bazungu's* [white men's] religion, and will go back to the religion of our fathers."

129

Of course the chiefs were delighted, for they boldly *"nyanzigged"* [bowed] when he finished speaking, clapping their hands, saying "I thank you!"

Mr. Mackay was asked why the missionaries had come to Uganda, and what they came to do. "We came," Mackay answered, "in response to the king's own request to Stanley, that he wished white men to come and stop with him, and to teach his people the knowledge of God."

"I understood that you came to teach us how to make powder and guns, and what I want is men who will do so," said the king, in a show of anger.

"We did not understand that. Our first work is to teach the Word of God, and how to read it."

"If to teach that is your main object, then you are not to teach any more. I want you to work for me."

Mackay replied, "We never have refused to do any work you have wished us to do; and everything the king has asked to be

130

done, I have done. There is scarcely a chief present for whom I have not done work."

He showed his hands, black with daily working in iron for those very chiefs who were saying the white men would not work for them.

"We want you to stop teaching to read, and to do work only for us and the king," shouted the chiefs.

"We came for no such purpose," replied the missionary. "If you wish that, then we cannot stay."

"Where will you go?"

"We shall go back to England."

Several hours were spent in such talk, and the court was again dismissed.

At last the time of the new moon had come and the following day was the wizard's great day of triumph. The missionaries did not go to the palace themselves; but, through a few of the more friendly natives, they learned what had happened. It was reported that four or five of the head chiefs had gone to the king and told him that if he did not receive the wizard and have the old religion back, they would take his throne from him and make one of his sons king.

Mr. Mackay writes: "Before dawn I was awakened by a terrible beating of drums in the neighborhood. I got up, and looked out in a dense fog. I gathered at once that it was the procession of the wizard going to the palace.

"The sound of drums got nearer, and the united shrill cries of hundreds of women became more distinct, and then faded away as the great procession turned up the highway to the king's palace. I felt relieved that the party did not have to pass our house, for who knows what a capricious and fanatical mob might have done on a moment's impulse? But I retired into my room with the feeling that we were in the hands of our loving Father, who will not allow a hair of our heads to perish.

"I afterward learned that the wizard put up at the house of Gabunga [head chief on the lake], who is now at the capital, till

132

midday, when he was received at the palace. The king was removed from his ordinary house, and seated in the main court, where the three huts were built for the wizard and his two companions. By some reports, Mutesa and his wives alone were inside the house, the katikiro sitting in the doorway, and all the other chiefs sitting outside, while the wizard also sat outside near the door, his companions sitting near him.

"All agree in saying that a vast quantity of beer was consumed by the wizard and chiefs, Mutesa scarcely touching the liquor; that the king sat silent all the time, while the wizard sang. Some say that Mutesa paid little attention to the wizard, but called forward the small sorcerers to play and dance before him. Few were near enough to know anything that the wizard said or sung; but one man says that he predicted war in the country from the presence of strangers, not now, perhaps, but within four or five years."

For several days the great wizard and his

companions presented themselves at court, going through their chanting, dancing, and drinking as on the first day. Finally, the last day of the year, Mutesa refused to see the wizard again because the cure which was expected had failed. Mukasa was obliged to leave and return to his island home.

So the year ended. King Mutesa had yielded to the persuasions of his chiefs and relatives and had returned to his old heathen ways only to be disappointed again by the false pretensions of the heathen wizard. What might next be expected no one dared to predict.

CHAPTER VII

THE TWO-FACED MUTESA AND THE MOHAM-
MEDANS

KING Mutesa had openly rejected both the religion of the white men and that of the Arabs, and declared himself again a worshiper of the heathen spirits. For him, however, it was as easy to change his religion as to change his clothes. Not more than two weeks after he had compelled his court to do reverence to the wizard, he said to his chiefs:

"Why are you not continuing to learn to read? You are all trying to gather riches for this world. You had better prepare for the world to come. Here are white men who have come far from Europe to teach you religion. Why do you not learn?"

He even went so far as to distribute many

reading sheets among his chiefs and pages. As a result, some who because of fear had ceased going to the missionaries' home, now renewed their visits, and others were made bold to begin to study for the first time.

Yet during the months which followed the wizard's visit, the missionaries were very much neglected by Mutesa. He no longer sent them presents of bananas, goats, and chickens, and their supply of cowry-shells for buying food became exhausted. Most of their clothes were either badly worn or had been pawned for food. They needed also oil for their lamps, paper for printing, and many other things not to be had in Uganda.

So in April, 1880, Mr. Mackay started on a journey to Uyui, several hundred miles south of the lake where were other English missionaries who had lately come from England with fresh supplies. Some thirty days, Mr. Mackay and his companions spent in "frail, tiny barks, made of rough hewn boards, sewed together with twigs," and another month was occupied in traveling overland to Uyui. During the time Mr. Mackay spent merely in going to Uyui, their nearest supply house, perhaps five hundred miles from Uganda, one could now make the trip from New York City to Shanghai, China, and return. This trip kept Mr. Mackay away from the capital for nine months, Mr. Pearson being the only Protestant missionary left in Uganda.

About three months after Mr. Mackay had left the capital, the fickle Mutesa again changed his religion. One night he dreamed that he saw ten moons and an eleventh which was both larger and brighter than any of the others. The big bright moon waxed more and more brilliant and grew larger and larger until the ten other moons came and bowed down before it. While Mutesa was wondering what the dream meant, he thought he saw two angels standing before him and he was frightened by their angry looks.

"Why have you and your court ceased to

137

pray the Mohammedan prayers?" one of the angels asked.

Now all Mohammedans are taught to pray five times a day. In order that every one may know just the time when the prayers should be said, a priest from the top of some high building calls loudly Arabic words, which mean "God is great. I bear witness that there is no god but God! I bear witness that Mohammed is the Prophet of God! Come to prayers! Come to prayers! Come to salvation! There is no other god but God!" Immediately, every good Mohammedan, no matter where he is or what his task, believes that his first duty is to wash his hands and kneel down to pray.

So the angel said to Mutesa: "If you wish to be prosperous and your land to grow, return at once to this old custom and call the people to prayer as the Koran commands."

On telling the dream to his wives, Mutesa was easily persuaded to think that he was like the large moon and that soon ten king-

"Come to Prayers! Come to Salvation!"

doms would come to him and beg him to rule over them.

On meeting his chiefs at morning *baraza,* the proud king repeated his dream to them also. Then and there, he commanded them all to obey the order of the angels and to pray, *"La-ilaha-illa-Allah, Muhammedun Rasul Allah"*—one of the creeds which Mohammedans are taught and which they repeat again and again. The Arabic words when translated mean, "There is no god but God; and Mohammed is the Prophet of God."

Mutesa's command needed merely to be given and the royal palace resounded with the prayers of scores of men who were ready to follow any religion their king might choose.

Mutesa announced that he himself was no longer a worshiper of the gods of Uganda or a follower of *Isa* [Jesus], but, from henceforth, his religion was that of Mohammed. In the church, within the royal enclosure where only a short while before men had

139

prayed to the Lord Jesus, now each day Mohammedan prayers were chanted. Every chief, wherever he might go, was accompanied by a boy carrying a mat and a kettle, so that when the call to prayer was heard, he might wash his hands and kneel on the mat in obedience to the Koran.

Some days after the public announcement of his new religion, Mutesa declared that since he had determined to follow the dream, he had been cured of his long-standing sickness. For some time he held *baraza* regularly in the grand style which had been habitual years before, but which was set aside after he began to suffer from his lingering disease. Soon, however, the malady proved as serious as before.

During this period when the Mohammedans enjoyed the royal favor, the Arabs gloried alike in their own power and in the seeming defeat of their enemies, the white men.

On Mr. Mackay's return from the southern end of the lake, they were ready to tell

140

the king the most unthinkable series of falsehoods about the missionary. These they hoped would further prejudice his mind against Mackay and cause Mutesa either to drive the white teacher from the country or to take his life.

At *baraza* one morning, when one Catholic priest and two Arabs were present, the crafty Mutesa, always eager to start exciting discussions at court, said: *"Makay milalu,"* ("Mackay is mad"). Having waited for just such an opportunity, the Arabs now boldly presented their charges.

They said that Mackay was a criminal of the worst sort; that he had fled from England because he had there murdered two men; that when he boarded the steamer bound for Africa, he carried two revolvers in his hands, with which he threatened to shoot the captain on the spot if he refused to take him to Zanzibar; that, from Zanzibar in turn, he was compelled to flee because of more murders he committed there; that in Unyanyembe he had walked about carrying two revolvers hoping for an opportunity to kill the governor; that it was very dangerous to allow him to remain in Uganda, for he was insane and only tried to murder people. They further declared that Mackay, being very much afraid that the story of his crimes would reach Mutesa's ears, had, on that very morning, given the speaker a present and on his knees had besought him not to make public the facts about his wicked life.

When the story of that morning's *baraza* was told Mr. Mackay, what were his thoughts? In his journal that night, these were some of the words he wrote:

"God is over all, and he is our God and our sole defense. In fever, when one's nerves are weak, many doubts arise in the mind, and through morbidly dwelling on the number of our bloodthirsty enemies, faith almost fails. Yet the fever subsides, and courage rises with better health, and one cannot but feel a deep inward, peaceful consciousness that, though we are absolutely shut off from every human help, yet we have protection more secure than any consul can afford, even the omnipotent arm of Jehovah.

"For the terrible charges laid against me, some proposed in court that I should be put to death. Even the charge of carrying my revolver is false, for I almost invariably march unarmed, having only my umbrella. Mutesa, however, said that the best thing to do was to send me home, as being a raiser of much noise and row in court. He knows very well that this charge, too, is unfounded. One of the French missionaries complimented me on the quiet manner in which I talked with Mutesa, while Arabs and others spoke loudly and excitedly.

"We now can understand to the full the meaning of that blessing which we are promised when men shall *revile* us, and persecute us, and shall *say all manner of evil* against us falsely for His sake. We are His, and it matters not what man can do to us."

143

The Arabs long continued to slander the missionaries in this way whenever it was possible to do so. They took advantage of the occasions when the missionaries were not at court to make false charges against them before the king.

One morning when a goodly number of them were present at *baraza,* they said, "The English are taking advantage of Mutesa's illness. Since you are unable to go about to see what is going on in your kingdom, the English are building a castle of clay which will become a fort; and they have many guns. When they finish building they will fight."

Mutesa answered: "The English are at Zanzibar and have not yet taken that place. Is it likely that they will begin fighting here when they have not yet 'eaten' any part of the coast?"

Failing in their charge against the English, the Arabs next attacked the Frenchmen. "Mapera has many guns," they said, "and has bought fifty slaves and is training

144

them to fight. Then they will make war."

Mutesa did not seem inclined to believe this charge either, and said that he knew that Mapera was not a fighting man. "I accept your religion," he said, "and do not want the religion of the *Bazungu* [white men]. Leave off then abusing them."

Pleased that he had professed to accept their faith, the Arabs began to flatter him because of his wisdom.

"The *Bazungu*," they said, "do not know how to pray. They never wash their hands before eating. They keep dogs which are unclean animals. Their skin is white because they eat swine's flesh. We eat only clean animals, we always wash before eating and before praying, and we pray regularly four and five times a day."

Mutesa again praised the Mohammedan religion and commanded all his chiefs to go immediately and pray at the mosque which had been put up on the palace grounds.

When they returned Mutesa asked: "Have not the *Bazungu* a book also from

145

which they pray? Is there no one present who can repeat their prayers for me to hear?"

Mufta being present was asked to read. He read the prayer beginning, "Our Father which art in heaven."

"There," cried the Arabs, "what is that? Allah is not our Father, and whoever saw him in heaven? Did we not tell you that these people do not know how to pray?"

The king then decreed that all should pray as the Arabs did, and that every one who was found not doing so should be caught and killed.

Later another discussion arose at court about the religions of Christ and Mohammed. Mr. O'Flaherty, who had taken Mr. Pearson's place in the mission, took the side of the Christians.

"In what does the wealth of Europe and Zanzibar consist?" asked Mutesa of one of the Arabs present.

The Arab mentioned houses, lands, cattle,

146

slaves, ivory, merchandise, pearls, gold, and silver.

"In what does the wealth of Uganda consist?" asked Mr. O'Flaherty of the king.

"Our riches," said Mutesa, "lie in ivory and women and cattle and slaves and houses."

Mr. O'Flaherty replied, "Ivory will by-and-by be all gone; your women die every day of the plague; your cattle get eaten up; your slaves die; and your houses, why I could set them all on fire with one match. What will you have then? All these things perish. I, therefore, advise you to seek the true riches which are above, and which cannot pass away. Seek first to know God and to love him with all your heart, and then you will have wealth which will last always."

"I want to have nothing to do with Jesus Christ," Mutesa replied. "I want goods and women. The religion of Jesus Christ will not give these to me, so I will not have it. The white men told me that God would protect those who read the Book. Smissi [Lieutenant Smith] was a man who read the book of Jesus Christ and he was killed. Does not Jesus Christ always abuse people? Did he not try to make the Jews accept his religion? But they would not have it, and killed him and scattered his followers. I don't want the *Bazungu* to come here with empty words. I want them to work and to bring me goods like the Arabs. If they will not make me ships and cannon, I do not want them. They tell me about God. Who ever saw God? Ask the *Bazungu* who ever saw God."

In answer, Mr. O'Flaherty asked Mutesa, "Did you ever see pain? Yet you have certainly felt it and know what it is. Did you ever see the wind? Yet you know it is here or there."

So the conversation continued. Mutesa's heart was bad and the missionaries were able to do little.

A few days later the Arabs invented another very cunning charge against the

148

English missionaries. Several of them, having called on the white men, had seen and heard their new music-box. So at court they told the king that Queen Victoria had sent him a fine music-box, but that the missionaries were keeping it for themselves. They further said that there were devils inside the box and when Mr. O'Flaherty whistled the devils began to play and when Mr. O'Flaherty said "stop," they were quiet. They also said that the Queen had sent Mutesa a thousand rifles, which they were also keeping for their own use. A hundred bales of cloth and many other things the Arabs said the missionaries were withholding from Mutesa. Of course, it was soon shown how false were all these charges.

After a long discussion about Jesus Christ, the Arabs broke out with a new attack. "The *Bazungu* are idolaters, they worship pictures."

Mutesa ordered a book brought which had been given him by the French Catholic priests. It contained a picture of God, the Father, as an old man with a long beard. The Arabs were delighted to have their charge seemingly proved true.

But the missionary was ready with a reply. "That is not really a picture of God," he said. "That picture has been made to help children to understand that God is our Father. But, you know that the Frenchmen and we do not agree on such things: we have the same faith in important matters, but pictures we don't believe in as they do."

The evil stories invented by the Arabs were sometimes so bad that they sound ridiculous. Mr. Mackay seemed to be more fiercely slandered than any of the rest. The Arabs even made up this very queer fable, which they tried to use to Mr. Mackay's harm:

"A certain king," they said, "had a favorite cat, which was reported to have one day eaten all the eggs. The king, however, said, 'It is my cat, let it alone; it must eat.'

150

Next day it was reported to have eaten the hens. 'Let it alone,' said the king, 'it is my favorite cat; it must eat.' After this it ate the goats, and then all the cows; but still the king would not let the cat be touched. Next it ate up all the people, and the king's wives, and then his children, and finally it ate up the king himself. Only one son of the king escaped by hiding himself. Meantime the cat grew and swelled to a great size, from having devoured so many things.

"But at length the one prince who escaped, succeeded in killing the cat. When he cut it open, he found all the eggs and the fowls and the goats and the cows and the people and the wives and the king's sons. But in the act of cutting the cat up, the prince accidentally wounded in the thigh one of his brother princes inside the cat. This fellow got out and said, 'What did you wound me for?' 'Do you not see,' said the other, 'that I have been doing you a good service in letting you out?' But he refused

151

to be at peace, and tried to kill the prince who had let him out!"

"The wonderful cat is the English," said the Arabs, "and the wounded prince who wished to kill his deliverer is Mackay. You, Mutesa, have conferred every benefit on him, but he means only to return you evil for good!"

"Could enmity and falsehood go further?" wrote Mackay in his journal. "But none of these things move me. The Lord has preserved me many a time from the hatred of these revilers and wicked men, who, for no reason at all, delight so to speak all manner of evil against me falsely. It was this very morning that Pearson and I read together at prayers the fifty-first chapter of Isaiah:

" 'I, even, I, am he that comforteth you: who art thou, that thou shouldest be afraid of a man that shall die, and of the son of man which shall be made as grass; and forgettest the Lord thy maker, that hath stretched forth the heavens, and laid the

152

foundations of the earth; and hast feared continually every day because of the fury of the oppressor, as if he were ready to destroy? and where is the fury of the oppressor? The captive exile hasteneth that he may be loosed, and that he should not die in the pit, nor that his bread should fail. But I am the Lord thy God, that divided the sea, whose waves roared: the Lord of hosts is his name. And I have put my words in thy mouth, and I have covered thee in the shadow of mine hand.'

"With such a promise, and such a refuge, and such a God, who shall be afraid? Lord God, give us more faith in thee! As for these Mohammedans and all others who speak so falsely of us, we would have no bitter feelings in our hearts against them. Lord, have mercy on them, and lead them to know thee, and then they will love thee and love thy servants."

Such a one, whose desire was best expressed in a prayer for his enemies, was a true Christian, for he was like his Master,

153

CHAPTER VIII

THE NEW TEACHING MAKES NEW MEN

OCTOBER the eighth, eighteen hundred and eighty-one, was a great day for the two English missionaries in Uganda. Mr. Litchfield and Mr. Pearson, having been compelled to return to their homeland, Mr. Mackay and Mr. O'Flaherty were at the time alone in the mission. The day brought nothing unusual but a letter addressed to Mr. Mackay.

The letter was short—very short—as it contained but two sentences. It was not beautifully written, for the writer had never had a lesson in penmanship. The pen used was a pointed piece of spear grass and the ink had been made from pot soot and plantain juice. None of us could have read it, for it was written in Luganda, yet it

154

brought Mr. Mackay the best news he had heard since reaching Uganda. During all the three years he had spent in Mutesa's kingdom, not a single black man or woman in the country, as far as he knew, had showed that he truly wanted to be a Christian. This little letter bringing the good news was from one of Mackay's first pupils, a young man named Sembera.

"Bwana [Master] Mackay," it read, "Sembera has come with compliments and to give you the great news. Will you baptize him, because he believes the words of Jesus Christ?"

Never afterwards was Sembera ashamed of being a Christian. Day by day, he lived the sort of life which convinced every one that he was "true blue." Although only a slave boy, he was ever trying to persuade others to become Christians. Two years after his baptism two young men whom he himself had won boldly acknowledged Jesus as Lord and Saviour; and even his old slave master became a Christian later, be-

155

cause Sembera his slave boy had taught him of Jesus.

About a month after Sembera's note came, another bit of important news reached the missionaries. A lame slave boy, named Dumulira, one of Mr. O'Flaherty's advanced pupils, was missed for some time from the daily reading class, and the missionaries did not know what the trouble could be. Later, when Mr. O'Flaherty was waiting in one of the courtyards of the palace, a lad stepped up and handed to him a Gospel, saying that Dumulira had asked that it be returned to the white man. His friend Dumulira, he said, was dead. He himself used to be a follower of the wizards, but now he no longer believed his old superstitions. To prove that he was honest, he showed Mr. O'Flaherty that he no longer carried any charm about his clothes.

The change in the heathen lad had come about at a time when hundreds of Waganda were dying of the plague. While Dumulira was sick, he asked his heathen friend to go

156

to the missionaries for medicine; but the heathen lad was afraid and would not go. All day long, the sick boy read from the Gospel of Mark, until his pains grew too intense to read longer, and soon afterward he died.

That day the heathen lad lost his faith in the evil spirits worshiped by the Waganda. Soon he, too, was one of the "readers" at the missionaries' school and was taught more about the Christ who had made his friend's death-bed so sweet.

About five months after Sembera's letter was received, the first five Christian Waganda then living were baptized by Mr. O'Flaherty. For this special service the missionaries' home was turned into a chapel. After the solemn and impressive ceremony of the morning was over, a bounteous dinner was served to about thirty lads and men and a goodly number of women besides, Mr. Mackay being the chief cook for the occasion. It was a very happy as well as a solemn day; and others, too, began to

157

think seriously of coming out boldly for Christ.

The five young men who were baptized had all been pupils in the white men's school for a long time, and had repeatedly expressed their determination to be followers of Jesus. To make every one feel that these young men were beginning a new life, they were given new names when baptized. Sembera was now called Sembera Mackay. Two of them had formerly been known by the name of the old wizard of the lake, Mukasa. One was now called Philipo for Mr. O'Flaherty, who was called Philipo by the black men; and the other was named Edwardo. The fourth was called Henry Wright, for one of the missionary secretaries in England; and the fifth was named Yakobo, meaning Jacob.

From this time on, the number of those who were earnestly seeking to learn how to follow the white man's religion steadily increased. Some walked three, four, and five hours to reach the missionaries' home.

"The Chief Teaching His Wives"

One faithful chief was obliged to wade through a swamp up to his waist in going from his home to that of the missionaries.

One day a chief came who said he had heard one morning at *baraza* the discussions between Mr. O'Flaherty, the king, and the Arabs; and he wanted now to hear more of what the white man had to say. Mr. O'Flaherty gave the chief his evenings, teaching him to read the Lord's Prayer, the Creed, part of the New Testament, and certain other Scripture verses. Occasionally he went to the chief's home to teach him. Calling one day at his hut, he was happily surprised to find the chief teaching his women or wives, some to say the alphabet, some to spell, and some to read the Lord's Prayer.

One morning, the man who had been the special wizard or priest for this chief came also to the missionaries' home. Many regular pupils and visitors, together with other wizards and worshipers of the spirits, were present. In the midst of the teaching, this

159

priest arose and knelt at the feet of Mr. O'Flaherty.

"I will cast off these charms of the spirits, whom I will never again serve," he cried. "They are liars and cheats. I will follow Jesus and learn his ways." On saying this, he cut off the valuable charms he carried about his person and took off his priest's robes and threw them all into the fire.

Soon after this the chief was ordered by the king to go to a distant part of the country. Having been away some months, he sent his converted priest back to the mission house, several days' journey, to ask for a prayer-book. It happened that when he arrived, another priest, richly robed and adorned with charms, was talking with Mr. Mackay. The heathen priest was describing his different kinds of charms; one he had to keep off lightning; one was to heal snake bites; and others were to heal various kinds of sicknesses. Mr. Mackay finally persuaded the man to allow him for a few

160

minutes to have one of his most precious charms which he carried on his head. On handing it over to the missionary the wizard cautioned Mr. Mackay not to place it on his head lest some dreadful calamity should be sent upon him by the god. This was the very thing Mr. Mackay did, at the same time addressing the crowd of Waganda. Expecting to see Mackay smitten dead on the spot, some of the people were so frightened that they ran away. The wizard himself seemed interested and convinced of the folly of his belief.

Then the converted wizard stepping forward boldly addressed the people. He told them how he had thrown all his charms and his priestly robes into the fire; for he had been led to believe in the Lord Jesus Christ, the Great High Priest of the true God. Those present were deeply moved, and many went away asking themselves, "Is not the Christian's God the true God?"

These interesting and encouraging things were happening while the Waganda every-

161

where were living in constant fear of death. The land was sorely stricken with the plague, much as Egypt was in the days of Moses. When this was at its worst, it seemed as though there was not a single house in Uganda where at least one had not died.

The disease snatched several from the noble Christian band. Two of these victims, young men of the king's household, were expecting to be baptized in a few months. When smitten with the plague, however, they were treated as were all others and carried off into the jungle and left to die. Some friend, learning of this, wrote a note to Mr. O'Flaherty, which read: "Hasten to such a place in Rubaga and bring with you some medicine, for your two friends are being carried away thither smitten with the plague."

Mr. O'Flaherty hastened to them, and found them alone in the deserted place; for those who had borne them to the jungle were afraid of being seized with the dread disease. There were a few words of cheer and a short prayer by the missionary. "I shall never forget," wrote Mr. O'Flaherty, "the look up to heaven by the first young man, Mukasa, and the words, among many others, to the effect that, although he was leaving an earthly palace, he was going to the palace in heaven; and turning to his friend he said, 'Jesus our Saviour is King.' His hands were clasped in mine, but in a paroxysm of burning agony he released his grasp and passed away. Turning to my other friend, I found him already in the throes of death, but I felt his name was entered on the Book of Life in heaven."

Another victim of the plague was Philipo Mukasa, one of the first five baptized by the missionary. For a long time he had been Mr. O'Flaherty's personal friend and helper. In the religious services he became the leader in the singing and in the responsive Bible reading, and in the school he was made one of the regular teachers. Once shortly after his baptism, he weakened under the tempting offer of his brother, a chief, who promised him a wife, the African's great desire, if Philipo Mukasa would only become his heathen priest. However, with his wife Sarah he soon returned to the missionaries, asking that both might be permitted to remain with them.

At all other times Philipo was true to his God. Even before he was baptized he had suffered persecution for the *Bazungu's* [white men's] religion. It was when Mutesa, because of his dream, had turned his court into a Mohammedan assembly. At the time Philipo Mukasa was the janitor of the church within the palace enclosure where the chiefs began to go regularly to repeat Mohammedan prayers. Philipo Mukasa refused to join them, and said that the religion of Jesus which the white men taught was the only true religion. When his words were reported to the king, the brave young man was put in the stocks; and shortly after he with another of the missionaries' pupils was sent off bound into the country.

164

On another occasion, after Philipo's return, Mr. O'Flaherty was too ill to attend court. The missionaries were being slandered by their enemies who said that they were bribing people to get them to come to read, and that they were running away with the palace women. The king ordered every pupil found about the premises to be caught, when Philipo Mukasa came heroically to their rescue. He pleaded the missionaries' cause so ably at court that, instead of being murdered for his boldness as he expected, the king and katikiro each gave him a present of cloth.

Philipo's wife, Sarah, grew to be as noble a Christian as himself. When first brought to the missionaries' home, she was a haughty savage who refused to touch the white men's food. "Can a woman learn?" she asked, when they tried to teach her. Soon however she became a good reader and, more than that, a most helpful person about the place. One day she was seen working in the garden with the other women.

165

"Sarah," asked the missionary, "who told you to work; I thought you were above working?"

"I cannot wash and sew like my white sisters in England," she answered. "I wish I could; but I can prune and hoe, and the plantains which feed us require both. It is my duty to assist in feeding this great family."

It was a sad night for her and all the Christians when Philipo Mukasa was smitten with the plague and died. His brothers came to take away the corpse, but the missionary and Sarah refused, saying that because they were Christians and Jesus was their elder brother, they were more closely related to Philipo Mukasa than his natural brothers. When his heathen relatives saw the fine grave the white men made and the beautiful bark cloth and the clean white linen in which they wrapped the dead body, they said: "You have buried him a chief; we also wish to be your brothers."

During the larger part of the year 1883,

Mr. Mackay was absent from Rubaga. He was trying to fit up a second vessel to take the place of the steam launch they had formerly used on Victoria Lake. His heart, however, was very much in Uganda, and he greatly wished to see these young Christians baptized and to help to train them for larger usefulness.

One interesting young man, Mwira by name, who came while Mr. Mackay was away, asked permission to stay with the missionaries. During the day, he worked for hours in the garden side by side with Mr. O'Flaherty; and at night, he had scores of questions to ask as the missionary tried to teach him of Christ. On returning to his home he was given some Christian books. After several months' absence he returned with his wife and babe, asking that his wife, too, might be taught to read. She had been with the missionaries only a day or two when she went to Mr. O'Flaherty to ask for a hoe that she might go and work in the garden and help to earn her own bread.

The missionary objected, saying: "Stay and learn, you are my guest; I'll feed you."

"How can I while you labor," she answered. "No, you stay with us, and teach us, and we will go and cultivate."

Unlike most Waganda husbands and wives Mwira and his wife loved each other. When baptized they chose for themselves the names Yohana (John) and Maryamu (Mary), from the two Bible characters they especially respected.

Before Mwira finally said good-by to the missionaries, he attempted to describe how he felt as a Christian man. This is about what he said.

"I am like a man traveling in a mountainous country. He climbs and passes ridge after ridge with pleasure. But as he surmounts each he looks before him to the heights beyond, each one loftier than those he has passed, and he becomes impatient, and wonders to himself if he will ever surmount the last. But there is one great difference. The traveler in his desire hastens from the summit of one ridge to descend, that he may climb another height; thence he hastens on till he climbs the last and highest. Not so I. When I climb I like to lie on the top and rest, and enjoy the others before me. Yes, I like to rest, and drink of the fountains that gush forth as I climb. Oh, the pleasure of reading and thinking upon these delightful books, and of meditating on the wonders of the Son of God becoming man to save men from evil spirits!"

So the number of Waganda Christians grew. Some were slaves, some were chiefs, some were officers of the king's household, and several were the king's own daughters. By October, 1884, eighty-eight Waganda had been baptized. Black men, women, and children were being born again with new hearts pure and white.

CHAPTER IX.

MACKAY'S QUEER NEW NAME

MR. MACKAY was not an ordained minister of the gospel, but a mechanic. His best sermons were preached by the things he made with his hands. His sunburned face told of the hours spent out of doors as farmer, carpenter, or bridgebuilder, and his hands were blackened and hardened by the heavy labor which was almost continually his. Many a time he longed for more spare hours in which the bright lads who came to the mission might be taught to read the Bible. At nights and in the evenings when out-door work was impossible, he would turn into schoolmaster, or printer, or, with the help of some Waganda boys, he would make an attempt at translating parts of the Bible into Luganda.

He wrote: "Any amount of mere preaching would never set these lazy fellows to work; and if only the slaves work, what better are matters than before? I have made work so prominent a part of my teaching that I am called *Muzungu-wa Kazi* [white man of work]. I tell them that God made men with only one stomach, but with two hands, implying they should work twice as much as they eat. But most of them are all stomach and no hands! That *I* work with my hands is a great marvel, and should be a healthful lesson."

During the year 1881 there was more than the usual amount of work to keep the hands of Mr. O'Flaherty and Mr. Mackay busy. Indeed the "white man of work" seldom could spare time to attend the royal *baraza*. Mr. O'Flaherty, being preacher, was the one who carried on the greater number of the discussions with the king and his chiefs at court.

Just now a good sized farm of perhaps twenty acres was at the disposal of the

171

missionaries—ten times as much as the king had given them at first. To raise for themselves all the vegetables, fruit, and stock they might need for food became their ambition. Thus they would no longer be dependent upon the favor of a fickle king for gifts of food and for cowry-shells to keep them from starvation.

It was no easy task to cut down the trees and underbrush and to break up the soil, so as to prepare these acres of wild land for cultivation. The natives never having been used to the idea of working for wages, all manual work being done by slaves, it was difficult to get men and women to help in this undertaking. At first the blacks would only beg and steal from the white men, whether any work had been done or not. Finally, the white men succeeded in getting a few helpers to agree to finish a certain piece of work for definite wages. Some would work a week for the payment of a very small quantity of cloth. Women, who in Uganda do all the gardening, came to hoe and prune the plantain trees for a few cowry-shells, while half grown lads sometimes consented for pay to do this woman's work.

After months of patient labor, fifteen hundred plantain trees were growing on the land. Splendid crops of maize, millet, wheat, beans, peas, tomatoes, and sweet potatoes were being gathered. There was a fair herd of cattle, together with goats and chickens—enough to supply them with meat. Part of the coffee they used was raised on their own trees, and the cotton they wove into cloth was of their own planting. From their own wheat crops they made flour and baked bread in a brick oven devised by Mr. Mackay. Plantain rinds were burned to make lye for soap-making. They even went so far as to make sugar and molasses from Uganda sugar-cane. All these new forms of labor the missionaries did themselves or taught the natives by patient example.

To all the tasks of various kinds involved in farming was added that of building a new home for the missionaries. Hitherto they had lived in a hut of native build. Oftentimes the rain would drip through the grass roof, and on the moist mud floors weeds and grass would insist on growing. The lower parts of the walls, being shaded by the roof and soaked by the rains, soon rotted. Because such conditions were so unhealthful, Mr. Mackay determined to build the best sort of house he could with the materials at his disposal.

Because of the rumors spread by the Arabs that brick houses would be used as forts, he did not dare build of that material. So the frame he made of wild palm, the only wood in Uganda which can resist the ravages of the white ants. Between the beams, the walls were filled in with stones and red clay and plastered over, both inside and outside, with plaster. To protect these walls from rain, the heavily thatched roof was made to extend some feet beyond them and was supported by substantial pillars. The two stories within and the stairway connecting them seemed most marvelous to the ignorant Waganda, who had never before seen one house built on top of another. The wooden floor and the lattice-work for windows did much toward making the house comfortable and wholesome as a home for the white men.

With all the delays caused by inefficient and lazy workmen, by Mr. Mackay's occasional attacks of fever, and by the dozen and one other hindrances that may not be named, a full year passed before the new home was completed. The fame of this wonderful house and farm spread even beyond the bounds of Uganda, and here and there some enterprising man began to copy this or that improvement suggested by the white man's way of living.

For three years the missionaries had been drinking the same kind of water as was used by the natives. Not a well or a pump had ever been seen in the land. The water which naturally drained into the hollow swamps between the hills, carrying filth

175

with it, was the only supply the Waganda knew. After a fearful plague had swept over the land and the white men themselves had been weakened by repeated attacks of fever, they realized the urgent need for a well of their own where they could find pure fresh water. They decided to dig a well within their own premises. The men who were set to work with pick and shovel could not believe that water could be found by digging into the top of a hill. Water could be found only at the bottom, they said.

"When we got too far down to throw up the earth with a shovel," says Mr. Mackay, "I set up a trestle of strong trees; and with rope and pulley and bucket, much to the astonishment of all the natives, we hoisted up the clay, till we reached water just at the depth I predicted. The Waganda never saw a deep well before, and would not believe that water could be had on a hillside until they saw the liquid itself. It took more than a week to sink the well; but when I afterwards repaired a battered pump

176

which I bought in London, and they saw a copious stream ascend twenty feet high, and flow and flow, as long as one worked the handle, their wonder and amazement knew no bounds.

"Makay lubare! Makay lubare dala!" was cried by all. [Mackay is the great spirit, he is truly the great spirit.] But I told them that there was only one great Spirit, that is, God, and I was only a man like themselves. To each company that came near I explained the action of the pump, some understanding best when I said that it was only a sort of elephant's trunk made of copper. To others I explained that it was only a beer-drinking tube on a large scale, with a tongue of iron that sucked up the water, as their tongues sucked up the beer from their gourds.

"Oh, the *Bazungu,* the *Bazungu!* they are the men; they can do everything; the Arabs and coast men know nothing at all; they can only draw water in the swamp where we get it ourselves; but, oh, *eh, eh,* Mackay is

177

clever, clever; the king will get them to carry him to see this wonderful thing."

Very seldom was the "white man of work" unwelcome at court when he had time to go. Because of the wonderful things he made he became very popular with the king. One day he brought to the court a diamond and showed the king how glass is cut. He also exhibited a yoke and explained how oxen are harnessed so that they may be used for drawing loads.

"There must remain nothing for white men to know—they know everything!" said Mutesa in his astonishment.

"We know yet only the beginning of things. Every year we make advances in knowledge," Mackay replied.

"Can Waganda ever become clever like the *Bazungu?*"

"Yes, and yet even more clever."

The king laughed and said; "I don't believe it." Of course, the chiefs laughed too, as they always did whenever the king laughed.

"Is it not the case," asked Mackay, "that the scholar usually becomes wiser than his teacher? The skill of the *Bazungu* to-day is much greater than their skill a year ago, while to-morrow they will improve on the wisdom of to-day. The pupil stands on the shoulders of him that taught him. He sees all that his master sees, and a great deal farther too." All seemed delighted with the idea. A few moments later, when court was dismissed, many of the chiefs heartily shook hands with Mr. Mackay.

The fame of the "white man of work" reached its climax when he successfully served as undertaker for the king's mother, Namasole. While she was ill with fever, she refused to take any of the white man's medicine, nor would she allow any one near her wearing calico or anything foreign, so wedded was she to her old heathen ways. The native witch doctors brought their charms to her bedside and chanted their prayers over her, but she only grew worse.

When she died, the drums at the palace

were loudly beaten to frighten away the "king of terrors" who, they feared, might escort her departed spirit into the unseen world. In Uganda, only the souls of kings and great men and women were supposed to live after death. Special care was therefore taken at royal burials to give the dead due honor; for their spirits were supposed to enter into certain persons who then became witches and had the power, if angry, to do great evil to men. The story of the coffin and the sermon he preached through its making, the "white man of work" himself will tell.

"The royal mourning lasted a month, during which time no work was allowed to be done in the land. No boat could start nor any one carry a load, until the queen was buried. But while others were resting, I was toiling hard night and day, for thirty days, for all were waiting for me.

"The morning after Namasole died, Mr. O'Flaherty and I went to court to pay our respects to the king. All the chiefs were clad in rags, and crying, or rather roaring, with their hands clasped above their heads. Mutesa determined to make a funeral to surpass in splendor any burial that had ever taken place in the country. Such is the desire of every king to outstrip his predecessors. Fifty thousand bark cloths were ordered to be levied in the land, besides some thousand of yards of English calico.

"Mutesa asked me how we buried royalty in Europe? I replied that we made three coffins, the inner of wood, the next of lead, and the outer of wood covered with cloth. I knew the custom of the Waganda in burying their kings. It is to wrap the body, after mummifying it, in several thousand bark cloths, and to bury the great pile in a huge grave, building a house over all and appointing certain witches to guard the grave for generations.

" 'Would you be able to make the three coffins?' Mutesa asked me.

"I replied, 'Yes, if you find the material.'

"He said he had no lead but he had a lot

181

of copper trays and drums which he would supply, if I could manufacture a coffin out of them.

"Frequently we had been twitted by the king at court for failing to work for him; accordingly I agreed to be undertaker, thinking it a small affair. But then the dimensions! Everything was to be AS LARGE AS POSSIBLE!! Immediately all the copper in the king's stores was turned out and sent down to our mission. Fine large bronze trays of Egyptian workmanship, copper drums, copper cans and copper pots and plates—all were produced, and out of these materials I was to make a coffin for the queen. All the skilled workmen were ordered to my assistance.

"Next morning I went off to Rusaka some three miles distant, to measure the body. Much objection was made by the royal ladies there at my going in to measure the corpse. But my friend Kyambalango was there, as master of ceremonies, and he explained that I was commissioned by the king. But I was somewhat taken aback on being told by some of the other chiefs that I should have measured not the corpse but the dimensions of the grave, and make the coffin to fit the latter. I told them there was not copper enough in the land to make a box larger than necessary; that if there was, I would willingly make a coffin as large as a mountain, but as it was, I could make the inner coffins to suit the body and the outer one as large as a house if they liked.

"In ten days' time we had finished the two inner coffins, the first being of wood, cushioned all inside with cotton wool, and covered all over, inside and out, with snow white calico, secured with a thousand copper tacks. Ornamental work I made by cutting patterns out of black and white pocket-handkerchiefs, and tacking them on. The copper box measured seven feet long by three feet wide and three feet high, shaped like a coffin. But the king's copper was enough for barely more than the lid and ends, so we had to supply for the sides four sheets of copper plate, which the king paid for at once in ivory, as we did not think well to give these away out of the mission's stores. We gave our workmanship and skill and time, besides the tools, and all the iron nails (no small quantity). We received copper wire as an equivalent for the copper tacks. Even the copper coffin we neatly lined all over inside with white calico tacked onto laths which were first riveted to the copper plate.

"It is needless to describe the worry and trouble we had, working late and early, and sometimes all the night. At every hour of the day pages were sent down to inspect the progress and ask when it would be done. The native workmen, especially the headmen among them, would do almost nothing, and generally spoiled what they did. They preferred sitting down all day smoking, and watching how I did. I was able to get some assistance, however, from several of the younger fellows.

"But even in the doing of a small piece

of work like this, which all granted was far beyond their own powers to accomplish, there must needs be an exhibition of jealousy and ill feeling on the part of some chiefs and Arabs.

"They told the king that we made the coffins small, much too small for Namasole, because we wanted the timber to finish our own house with; that we had already secreted in our house a lot of boards; that perhaps we might show good workmanship, but we could not work fast.

"Mutesa alone stood our friend. He refused to believe that we had appropriated any boards, while he said to our accusers that what was done well could not be done in a day. 'Can a woman cook plantains well if you hurry her?' asked the friendly king.

"In a week's time we had about a hundred boards cut and squared to fit, and nailed together with strong ribs like the sides of a schooner. When together, it looked like a small house, rather than a

185

coffin. After a few more days, we had enough boards for the lid. Then we covered the whole outside with native bark cloth, and lined the inside with pure snow-white calico. Each side was made a piece by itself so that it might be easily carried. A thousand men arrived to bear the parts to the grave, and most fortunately it did not rain. We put them together before the king, who challenged all to say if such workmanship could be done in the country by Waganda, or if anything of the kind had ever been seen in the land.

"Next day we had the king's orders to go to the burial. He wanted us to go the same day, but we were too tired, having for a full month been constantly at saw and hammer from dawn to midnight, and often later.

"The grave was a huge pit, some twenty feet by fifteen feet at the mouth, by about thirty feet deep. It was dug in the center of the late queen's sleeping-house—a monstrous hut some one hundred and fifty feet in diameter. The monster pit was neatly

186

lined all round with bark cloth. Into this several thousand new bark cloths were thrown and carefully spread on the bottom filling up the hole a long way. Then the sides of the huge box were lowered in with much trouble. I descended and nailed the corners together.

"After that I was summoned to the ceremony of putting the corpse into the coffin. Thousands of women were there, yelling with all their might, and a few with tears in their eyes. Only the ladies of the royal family and the highest chiefs were near the corpse, which by this time was reduced to a mummy by constantly squeezing out the fluids with rags of bark cloth. It was wrapped in a new cloth, and laid on the ground. The chiefs half filled the nicely padded coffin with bleached calico; then several bundles of petty charms belonging to the queen were put in; after that, the corpse; and then the coffin was filled up with more calico.

"Kimbugwa, Kauta, and the other chiefs

in charge, carried the coffin to the court, where the grave-house was, when much more yelling took place. I screwed the lid down, but such was the affection of some of the royal ladies for the deceased that I had to have them ordered away, because of their crying and tears and hugging of the coffin, before I could get near to perform my duties as undertaker.

"Then came the copper coffin, into which the other was lowered by means of a huge sheet. The lid of that had to be riveted down, and that process was new to the chiefs standing by. 'He cuts iron like thread!' they said, as the pincers snapped the nails. 'Mackay is a proper smith!' they all shouted.

"With no mechanical contrivances, it was astonishing how they got the copper coffin, with its ponderous contents, lowered into the deep grave without letting it fall end foremost into the great box below. The task was effected, however, by means of the great multitude of men.

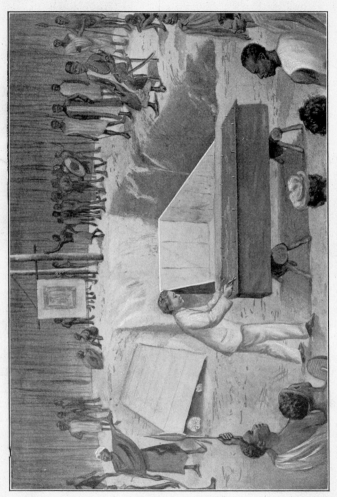

"He Cuts Iron Like Thread!"

"Thousands of yards of unbleached calico were then filled in round and over the copper coffin, until the big box was half full. The remainder was filled up with bark cloths, as also all the space round the outside of the box. The lid was lowered, and I descended once more to nail it down. Several thousand more pieces of bark cloth were then laid on till within three feet of the surface, when earth was thrown in to the level of the floor.

"We returned at dusk, but the burying was not completed till nearly midnight. Next morning, every man, woman, and child in the land had their heads shaved, and put off their mourning dress of tattered bark cloth and belts of plantain leaves. The country had been waiting till we were done with our carpentry."

In the grave of Queen Namasole that day, it is said, there was buried seventy-five thousand dollars' worth of bark cloth and calico. A more splendid burial had never before been given to royalty in Uganda.

189

King Mutesa was proud to think that in his kingdom so wonderful a piece of work was possible. Mackay had won his good will as never before, and was longing and praying that at last he might be used to win Mutesa's heart for the Lord Christ.

It was shortly before Christmas that his great opportunity came to plead with the king. This is the story of what took place as Mackay tells it.

"In the king's *baraza,* strangers were called forward to describe burial customs in vari ius parts of Africa and Arabia. Some told of burying scores of living virgins with a dead king; others told of how human lives were offered as sacrifices on like occasions; while others told of the pomp and ceremony displayed at funerals.

"Turning to Mackay, the king asked; 'Tell me how they bury in your country? Do they do aṣ I did in burying Namasole? Did you see any human sacrifices then?'

"Masudi (an Arab) began to describe to me how when Mutesa's grandfather died, his father had thousands slaughtered at the grave.

"'Don't mention such things,' I said to Masudi, with such a gesture of horror that he became quiet at once; 'they are too cruel to be spoken about before the Mutesa of to-day. You, Mutesa, far surpass any one, not only in Africa, or in Arabia, or in India, but even in Europe itself. I never heard of so much valuable cloth being buried in a royal grave as you buried with Namasole.' This, of course, pleased him, as black men are fond of flattery. 'But let me tell you that all that fine cloth and those fine coffins will one day all be rotten. It may take ten years, or may be a hundred years, or it may be a thousand years; but some day all will be rotten, and the body inside will rot too. Now we know this, hence in Christian countries we say that it matters little in what way the body is buried, for it will rot some time or other; but it matters everything what becomes of the soul. Look at these two head chiefs of yours sitting by you.

191

The katikiro is your right hand and Kyambalango is your left hand. They are both very rich. Next to you they are the greatest in the kingdom. They have cloth and cattle and lands and women and slaves— very much of all. Here they have much honor, and when they die they will be buried with much honor, but yet their bodies will one day rot.

" 'Now let me have only an old bark cloth, and nothing more of this world's riches, and I would not exchange my place for all the wealth and all the greatness of both the katikiro and Kyambalango. All their greatness will pass away, and their souls are lost in the darkness of belief in the wizards, while I know that my soul is saved by Jesus Christ, the Son of God, so that I have riches that never perish which they know nothing about.'

"The katikiro, evidently struck by my contempt of all his greatness, replied that Mutesa was a believer in Jesus Christ, while he was a servant of Mutesa, consequently he was a Christian. Mutesa then began his usual excuses.

" 'There are these two religions,' he said. 'When Masudi reads his book, the Koran, the white men call it lies; when the white men read their book, Masudi calls it lies. Which is true?'

"I left my seat, and going forward to the mat on which the katikiro was sitting, I knelt on it, and in the most solemn manner, I said, 'Oh, Mutesa, my friend, do not always repeat that excuse! When you and I stand before God at the great day of judgment, will you reply to Almighty God that you did not know what to believe because Masudi told you one thing and Mackay told you another? No, you have the New Testament; read there for yourself. God will judge you by that. There never was any one yet who looked for the truth there and did not find it.' "

So Mackay pleaded with Mutesa. Never again did another opportunity come. Like Agrippa in the days of Paul, this black king did not heed the Christian plea. His health grew worse continually. Weak and suffering intensely, he was unable to hold *baraza*. Two years after his mother's pompous funeral, he too died, and died a heathen.

CHAPTER X

THREE BOY HEROES AND ONE BOY TYRANT

BUSY writing home letters, one night in October, 1884, Mr. O'Flaherty for hours had been the only one astir in the missionaries' home. From his upstairs window, in the midnight stillness, he heard some one below softly calling his name, "Bwana Philipo! Bwana Philipo." Slipping down stairs, he found a native Christian with a friend, who under cover of the night had run to break the news which the missionaries had long dreaded to hear.

"King Mutesa is dead," they said, "fortify yourselves; the mission house will probably be plundered, and who knows how many may be murdered?"

Mr. O'Flaherty returned to the house and woke Mr. Ashe, who shortly before had ar-

rived as a new missionary in Uganda. Mr.
Mackay was down at the port on the lake,
twelve miles away, overhauling the new mission boat. As the two men talked and
prayed together, seeking to know the wisest
step to take, now and again the quick beat
of drums was heard, while every gust of
wind sweeping across the valleys bore the
weird cries of the palace mourners.

Judging from the amount of wailing at
court, one might suppose the late monarch
had been greatly beloved by his subjects;
but a glance behind the scenes before his
death might have led to a different opinion.
The direct cause of Mutesa's death will
never be known. Some said that the Arab's
medicine had proved to be a poison instead
of a cure, while others reported that the
king had been smothered to death by some
of his own wives. If either of these reports
be true, we may be sure that those who took
his life were among the loudest mourners.

It was an anxious night for all who had
heard the news. For generations, the death

of a monarch in Uganda had been the signal for robbery and bloodshed. People, sometimes to the number of two thousand, had been captured in the highways and offered as sacrifices at the grave of the dead ruler. Until the chiefs met and chose a new king from among the sons of the late monarch, no one was sure of his life. Upon the crowning of the fortunate prince, all his brothers who had been held as prisoners would be slain except the eldest, who according to Uganda custom, never sat on the throne. The old chiefs who had elected the new king were then usually deposed and some of them beheaded; while the young ruler chose new chiefs and new court officers. Until the young king was well established on his throne, Uganda usually was a land full of murder and thievery.

So on the death of King Mutesa, the missionaries feared the usual cruelties. Although Mutesa had not been to them always a faithful friend, yet they realized that it was his protection which had kept the jealous chiefs and Arabs from driving them from the land long ago. What was there now to keep a bloodthirsty mob from attacking them, from burning their houses, from plundering their gardens, and from sending them out of the country or perhaps torturing them to death? And would their faithful Christians have to suffer with them? With these thoughts of possible danger, the missionaries prayed to the Father; and trusting in his protection, they waited for the morning.

Early the next day, two messengers arrived from Mr. Mackay who, when they left the lake, had not yet heard the news. The men, having been robbed of their clothing on the way and compelled to flee for their lives, were in a sorry plight on reaching the missionaries' home. In the meantime, Mackay worked hard all day at the boat. At sundown when he was about to have his supper of plantains, he saw the people of the place coming toward him armed with shields and spears. On hearing the all-important news, he immediately launched the mission boat so that the entire party might quickly escaped if the mission house was burned, as those who reported the king's death assured him it would be.

But thanks to the katikiro, who became the ruler until the new king was chosen, the slaughters and thefts which all expected, were checked. Probably some lives were taken, but these were comparatively so few that the missionaries knew nothing of them until later. In the council of the great chiefs, the question was debated whether or not both the missionaries and the Arabs should be attacked. In this council, some were eager to rush at once to the plunder; but it was the word of the katikiro which held them in check and which saved the lives and property of the foreigners from the hands of their enemies.

But who was to be the new king? The people waited breathlessly for the decision of the council of the great chiefs. When the announcement was made, a great cheering arose from the palace, and some Christian boy escaped from the crowd unnoticed and ran to tell the news to his white friends.

"Mwanga alide Buganda." (Mwanga has eaten Uganda), he said.

To the missionaries this seemed good news. Mwanga was a lad about eighteen years of age who looked more like his father than any of his brothers. During Mutesa's reign, he had occasionally visited the missionaries and had learned a little of reading.

"If you should become king on your father's death, how will you treat us?" Mr. Ashe had once asked him when the boy was paying a visit to the missionaries.

"I shall like you very much, and show you every favor," was the reply.

However, it spoiled Mwanga to be made king of Uganda. During Mutesa's lifetime, his sons had no power, living lives but little better than those of the ordinary blacks; now, while still only a boy, Mwanga was made the great king of Uganda, and he knew no one in all the world so powerful as himself.

So sudden a change was enough to turn the head of a stronger man than Mwanga. He began to show all his father's weaknesses without any of his strong points. Instead of being the real ruler of Uganda, he soon became the slave of his katikiro. Mwanga seemed always afraid to do what he knew was right; and, when urged by his katikiro and chiefs to do wrong, he always proved too weak to say "no." The katikiro, the same man that held the position in Mutesa's reign, along with certain of the chiefs hated the missionaries exceedingly, and it did not take long for Mwanga to catch their spirit and to be ready to follow their leading.

First, Mwanga, wanting to impress the missionaries by his new power, haughtily refused to see them when they first called to pay him their respects. Somewhat disheartened by this first reception, the missionaries did not venture again to the court until some days later; and for this neglect they were chided by Mwanga.

The second day after Mutesa's death was announced, the "white man of work" was called from repairing his boat by the chiefs who found they could not build the dead king's coffin without the help of the white men. As soon as this work was completed, Mackay returned to the lake shore. While he was absent from the capital, his enemies busied themselves circulating slanderous reports about him. They said that, having slept in the boat at night, he came ashore in the morning and stole the people's plantains and goats. The fact of the matter was that the boat was beached at the time, receiving a coat of paint, and Mackay was ill with fever in his tent.

Mwanga had not long been king when the rumor was brought to his court that an army of white men was marching to Uganda by way of the land of Usoga. Usoga was a country just east of Uganda, the only neighbor of which the king was really afraid.

202

For generations the prophecy had been handed down among the Waganda that some day Uganda would be "eaten up" (conquered) by enemies entering the country from the eastern side through Usoga, the "back door."

Now, there were many reasons to make Mwanga begin to think that the foreigners who were coming were enemies. He had heard of fighting on the part of the English in Egypt to the north. News reached him that the Germans (to him the same as the English), were fighting for land in the region of Zanzibar; after gaining their prize there, he expected them to march inland, conquering as they came. In addition, he had been told of English and Germans who were living at the southern end of Victoria Lake. Now, worst of all, there was an army of white men in Usoga. Surely, the Englishmen already in Uganda were part of this great force and, after having gathered a large number of followers in his kingdom, they would unite with the

203

army in Usoga and "eat up the land." A
spark was all that was needed to fire these
suspicions. This spark was supplied by
Mujasi, the captain of the king's body-
guard, who had long been a bitter enemy of
the missionaries.

One day Mujasi noticed a lad, formerly
a follower of his, repairing the missionaries'
fence. He complained to the katikiro that
the white men were ruining the country,
that they paid men to work for them, so
that the chiefs like himself could no longer
get workers for nothing. A few days later,
several Christian lads, the servants of a certain chief, attended the communion service
on Sabbath at the mission instead of thatch-
ing a roof for the chief. Because of this
complaints were made.

Mwanga's mother hearing of what had
happened, exaggerated the report by saying
to the katikiro that no chiefs could get
work done, because the missionaries were
inducing hosts of people to serve them with
the purpose of raising an army of rebellion.

Mujasi also added the charge that every time Mackay crossed the lake, he took hundreds of Waganda with him. All these complaints together with the story of the white men in Usoga prepared the way for the first terrible crisis which broke out a few days later.

Mr. Mackay, having finished repairing the boat, gained permission from the king and the katikiro to go to Msulala at the southern end of the lake in order to take letters for home friends to a place where they would be carried on to the coast. About ten o'clock the next morning, the party started on the twelve mile walk to the port. The crew carrying the baggage and boat's gear, five or six of the schoolboys together with Mr. Mackay and Mr. Ashe, made up the company.

The boys and the crew with the loads went ahead, the two missionaries bringing up the rear. While on their way, a rumor reached them that Mujasi was out with a large army. As they walked along, every now and then they met companies of men, armed with spears, hurrying past them. Recognizing one of the men, Mr. Mackay asked him where the soldiers were going. He looked a little confused but replied that they had been ordered by Mujasi to capture some of the king's women who had run away. The company walked on until they were within a couple of miles of the lake. They were just entering a bit of scrubby forest, when a force of several hundred men headed by Mujasi himself sprang upon them. Armed with guns, spears, and shields, they shouted, "Go back! go back!"

"We are the king's friends, we have received the king's leave. How do you dare to insult the king's guests?" the missionaries asked as they tried to proceed. At this the crowd rushed upon them, snatching from them their walking sticks, their only weapons, and jostling them about in every direction. Mackay and Ashe did not attempt to fight, but calmly sat down by the side of the path.

"Where are you going?" demanded Mujasi.

"We are going to the port, having been given the permission of the king and katikiro."

"You lie," he replied. "Where is the Waganda messenger to go with you?"

"We have none," was the answer.

Again the crowd of warriors rushed upon them, pulled them to their feet, and pointed the muzzles of their guns right at the white men's breasts. The captives, however, said nothing, but quietly abandoning the trip to the lake, they reversed their steps, thinking this was merely a mad freak of Mujasi's, and never suspecting that he was acting under the king's orders. The mob continued to yell at them, to mock and to abuse them with the most offensive language, until they tired of hearing their own voices, seeing that the missionaries walked quietly on.

When they finally came to the point where two roads met, one leading directly to Mengo, Mwanga's new capital, the other to the missionaries' home, they halted until the crew and the five Christian boys overtook them. The crew, after being robbed of their guns, were freed, while the five Christian boys were marched along with their hands bound. The missionaries were then told to go back to their own home, and the Waganda boys under guard were marched off to the capital. It was now three o'clock in the afternoon, and the missionaries had been walking for five hours. Wearied and disappointed, they sat down to consider what should be done next. Mr. Ashe tells the story of what then happened:

"We decided to lose no time, but to lay the whole matter at once before the katikiro. When we reached his enclosure, we were bidden to wait. No one dared to announce our presence to the katikiro, as Mujasi was having a private interview with him, reporting his success in the late encounter. After waiting some time, we got up and went to the doorway, and Mackay called out loudly, 'Katikiro, my friend. I

am your friend. We are the white men.'
After calling once or twice, we were admitted and invited inside the house.
Mackay stated our case and asked why we
had been so badly treated."

To the surprise of the missionaries, the
katikiro merely smiled and said that Mujasi had turned them back because he found
them taking Waganda out of the country.
Mackay assured him that nothing of the
kind had been done.

"Oh, yes, Mujasi has caught five," insisted the katikiro.

Just then another case came on for hearing and the subject was dropped. As soon
as possible, Mackay insisted on their returning to the case about which they were most
concerned, and told the katikiro that it was
not right for them to treat their guests as
they had done.

"You are always taking away our people
and returning with hosts of white men and
hiding them in Usoga with the intention of
eating up our country," he cried.

209

Suddenly with flashing eyes, he turned to Mujasi and said: "To-morrow morning take your army and tie up Philipo and this other man, Mackay, and drive them back to the country from which they came."

Mr. Ashe says: "Mackay and I were utterly taken aback and astounded at this decision, and we begged the katikiro to hear us, and tried to take his hand to plead once more. But he waved us scornfully aside, and, with a cry of triumph from Mujasi's soldiers, we were hustled and dragged from the great man's presence, a dangerous and angry mob momentarily growing thicker about us. Soon they were actually quarreling for our clothes. 'Mine shall be his coat,' shrieked one; 'Mine his trousers;' 'No mine!' and there was a scuffle to get nearer the clothing they coveted. However, the katikiro did not wish matters to go quite so far, and sent his head executioners to warn off the vulture soldiers. The order was instantly obeyed, and dazed and amazed we found ourselves alone. It was now near sunset and we made our way back home in a very unhappy frame of mind."

In the quiet of their home, the missionaries knelt together and poured out their hearts in prayer to the Heavenly Father, trusting in his protection and asking for his guidance. It grieved them to think that the work of the mission might be suddenly ended; yet it looked as though the katikiro and Mujasi meant to kill every one they might find who had come to the missionaries to learn.

Fortunately some cloth was still left in the house. This they finally decided to turn into presents. Six loads were sent to the king, six to the katikiro, and one to Mujasi, with the hope and prayer that their anger might be calmed. The katikiro graciously accepted his gift, sending back word that again they would be brothers. Since the palace gates were closed for the night, the king's gift was returned with the message that the king would receive it in the morning. Mujasi, too, accepted his load; but sent word that he was collecting a force to rob them in the morning and burn their house; but seeing they had sent presents to the king and katikiro also, he would await further orders.

The missionaries urged all their Waganda servants and pupils who stayed on their premises to flee for their lives. One boy, however, Seruwanga by name, would not go. Mr. Ashe finding him asked him what madness it was which made him linger when in such danger. "I am going, my friend," he answered; but, alas, it was too late. That evening he, too, was captured. During the night, under cover of the darkness, two Christian young men ventured to come to the missionaries' home to tell them of their sympathy and loyalty. The next day Mujasi came and searched the house for Waganda Christians, but none were found.

For some reason, all but three of the boys captured the day before were released; but in the afternoon the report reached the missionaries that Mujasi was going to burn to

death the three who were still bound. None
can express the grief the missionaries felt.
They loved the boys as they would have
loved their own children. One of them,
Seruwanga, was going to die because he had
lingered too long in the mission premises.

The second, Kakumba, used to be the page
of a powerful chief. On his master's death
he had expressed the wish that he might
come and be the missionaries' servant instead of belonging to any other chief. So
he had been allowed to live in the missionaries' household.

The third, Lugalama, the youngest of all,
was a handsome young boy of twelve, who,
some years before, had been carried away
from his home as a captive in war. Having
fallen into the hands of Sebwato, a Christian chief, he was finally given his freedom
and sent to Mr. Ashe to be cared for. The
boy became a true friend of the missionary
and a general favorite about the mission
grounds.

These three boys, the oldest fifteen and

the youngest twelve, were to be burned to death by the savage Mujasi merely for the crime of having lived with the white men. The missionaries did everything they could to save their boys; but all efforts were in vain.

The sorrowful story was afterwards told to Mr. Ashe by Kidza, a Christian who as Mujasi's guide had witnessed the cruel scene. This is the account as Mr. Ashe gives it:

"Lugalama and Kakumba, when first arrested, were taken into a house, and Kakumba was beaten in accordance with a common Uganda custom in the treatment of prisoners. They had compassion on Lugalama and gave him some food. Next day they were taken to the king's enclosure and their sentence was pronounced, Mujasi being the chief accuser. Lugalama's former master tried to save him, but in vain.

"So the three boys, Seruwanga, Kakumba, and Lugalama, were led away to death, a mocking crowd following them.

" 'Oh, you know *Isa Masiya* [Jesus Christ],' said Mujasi. 'You know how to read.' 'You believe you will rise from the dead?' 'Well, I shall burn you and see if it be so.'

"These were some of the mocking taunts which they endured, and loud was the laughter which greeted such sallies. But the young Christians, as some reported, answered boldly and faithfully. Seruwanga was a daring fellow, and I can well believe that when Mujasi mocked he would sing a song they often sang at the Mission, *'Killa siku tuusifu'* ['Daily, daily sing the praises']. Kakumba, too, had come to the missionaries when all others were afraid, and perhaps his voice joined in the song. But what could have been in poor little Lugalama's heart but the haunting, overmastering horror of death—and such a death! There were none who dared to beat upon their breasts and show the sorrow that they felt, though there were many sympathizing friends who followed, many compassionate

215

hearts that God had touched with a pity which perhaps before they had never known.

"The mob, carrying gourds full of banana-cider, found their way toward the borders of a dismal swamp. Here they halted. Part of the crowd brought fire-wood, others made a kind of rough frame-work, under which the fuel was heaped. Then the prisoners were seized, and a scene of sickening cruelty was enacted. Some laid hold of Seruwanga, others of Kakumba, and others of Lugalama, brandishing their long, curved knives. Seruwanga committed his cause to Him who judgeth righteously, and the cruel knife could not wring from him a cry; bleeding he was cast into the fire. Kakumba appealed to Mujasi. Mujasi believed in Allah [God], the All-merciful—he pleaded a relationship with him; but, alas! there is as much mercy in the knife in the executioner's hand as in Mujasi's heart, and he too underwent the short agony and the flame.

"And now the saddest scene of all. Mu-

"Part of the Crowd Brought Fire-wood"

jasi bade them treat Lugalama as they treated the others. They came nearer, and he cried out, 'Oh, do not cut off my arms; I will not struggle—I will not fight! Only throw me into the fire!' Surely this was one of the saddest prayers ever prayed on this sad earth—'Only throw me into the fire!'

"The butchers did their work and marred what was so wonderfully made, and the poor bleeding boy was placed on the framework that the slow fire might finish what the cruel knife had begun. A wail of anguish went up, becoming fainter and fainter—a last sob, and then silence.

"Kidza stood sadly watching the sorrowful scene, wondering perhaps whether his turn might be next, when Mujasi, drunken with blood, came to him. 'Ah, you are here! I will burn you too and your household. I know you are a follower of *Isa* [Jesus]' 'Yes, I am,' said Kidza, 'and I am not ashamed of it!' Mujasi then left him."

"What shall I say of that day of waiting, hoping, praying, fearing—praying not vainly, though at the very time the awful deed was being done?

"Such prayers are not vain as they may seem, but the answer to them is yet to come. That was a day when the wrongs of Africa came home to me and burned themselves deep into my very soul—that day when Lugalama fell asleep, January thirty-first, 1885."

CHAPTER XI

A FTER the death of the three Christian
boys, Mujasi set a guard about the
mission premises and announced that he
would burn alive every person who had
adopted the white man's religion. He presented to the king and katikiro a long list
of those who he thought should be killed;
but, surprised at seeing the names of certain
prominent officers among the rest, the katikiro cried: "What, will you kill chiefs,
too?" and Mujasi was thereupon compelled
to cease his troubling. Soon the guard
about the mission premises was removed;
and, for a time, Mwanga's thirst for blood
seemed quenched.

The white men scarcely knew, however,
when to expect the storm again to break.

219

If the missionaries were taken away or killed, what would become of the little Uganda church of about a hundred members? Hitherto the Christians had always met in the mission house for worship. It was the missionary who led in the service, and it was he who did most of the teaching. To the missionaries the Christians came for advice when in difficulty; and to the missionaries they looked for encouragement when disheartened. If the missionaries were gone, would these Waganda stand by their Christian colors?

To help them to be more independent in the time of trial two things were done. First, out of their own number certain men were elected as leaders or elders. In the homes of these men the Christians of the neighborhood would gather quietly to worship or to study reading, when it might not be safe to meet in the missionaries' home. These elders were taught by the white men how to lead in worship, and were encouraged to be worthy helpers to the others.

220

The second thing done was made possible by the very persecutions they were enduring. For some time after the terrible murder, only a few pupils dared to venture to the mission house. The missionaries, being relieved of much of their teaching, gave their time largely to translating and printing. Not even one entire Gospel, as yet, had been translated into the Luganda language. All the Bible the Waganda Christians had (except a few who could read the coast language) was a few pages of Matthew and short selections chosen here and there from the Old and New Testaments. If their white teachers were driven from the country, how could the young Christians be expected to keep true to their Saviour, when they had so little opportunity to learn about him? For months, both by day and by night, the missionaries with the help of a small band of the more intelligent Christians toiled away at the translation of Matthew's Gospel into Luganda.

No "readers" being arrested for some

months, the Christians, and pupils who were not Christians as yet, gradually lost their fear and began to flock to the mission as before. Frequently, the school room and the new chapel were crowded to their utmost.

Strange to say, Mackay because of his mechanical skill again became popular at court. One morning on going to *baraza*, he was very much surprised to have the katikiro take him warmly by the hand and say that now Mackay was a favorite, and might have the katikiro's daughter for a wife. For a reply, Mackay merely asked him how long his favoritism would last.

"The king was very gracious," said Mackay, "expressing the hope that our former good relations were again restored. I told him that it seemed unreasonable that he and his people should value so highly our goods and workmanship, while he would not listen to what we said about the soul. The king said I was right, and the katikiro also said that we 'white men were evidently men of truth, for our cloth measured exactly as stated. A box of powder held the proper number of tins, with no sand mixed to adulterate it, and our guns fired without exploding and killing the purchasers, while Arab traders in salt mixed ashes in it to adulterate it and make it look more!' "

For some weeks Mackay had frequent talks with the king, not hesitating to charge him plainly with the terrible crimes committed in the king's name. Mwanga, however, continued to declare his friendship, saying one day: "I will never let you leave me; and while I live, and my son's son lives, I am determined to have white men in my country."

Yet only a few months later, or by the close of 1885, Mwanga showed himself a very different sort of king. The cruel part of his nature was awakened. Again reports came that an enemy was entering Uganda through the land of Usoga and would "eat" the country. A white general with a large following was already at the

223

country's "back door." He and his army were being held as prisoners by the chief of that region who was awaiting Mwanga's orders.

The fact really was that the white man about whom such swelling words were spoken was not the general of an army, but a missionary, the newly chosen bishop for Central and Eastern Africa. Utterly ignorant of the long-standing prejudice against entering Uganda through Usoga, Bishop Hannington had taken what seemed to him the shortest and easiest road from the coast. The missionaries in Uganda had written him a letter warning him of the danger, but he had never received it. They had endeavored to explain to Mwanga that the bishop was only a teacher of God, like themselves, and had not thought of eating the country, but the chiefs persuaded his majesty to treat all white men as enemies.

One day a page of the king secretly told the missionaries that Mwanga had sent an order to kill the bishop and all his men.

They hurried to the court to plead that messengers be sent to cancel the order; but for one excuse and another, Mwanga day after day refused to see them until it was too late, and a heathenish crime was committed at Uganda's "back door."

In the land of Usoga, on the eastern border of Uganda, Bishop Hannington for seven weary days was kept a prisoner in a dark, filthy hut. On the eighth day, Mwanga's messengers arrived and bade him come forth from his prison. He staggered out, pale and worn with the fever which had wrecked his body during the week of awful suffering in prison. Mr. Ashe tells the story as he heard it later from the lips of one who witnessed the dreadful tragedy.

"One of the messengers snatches up his Bible," he says, "another his portfolio, and another his sketch-book; and they lead him out, telling him he is soon to join his men."

"After two hours' walking, the party reaches an open space beyond the banana groves, where at last Hannington sees his

225

men, not, as he expected, with their loads,
nor carrying their guns and full of spirits
at the thought of once more being on the
road, but all bound, some with a heavy-
forked branch round their necks, and many
with their hands tied behind their backs.
They now see their master led into the open
where they are. He seems wonderfully
calm and turns as if to sit down—but this is
not allowed. A gun is fired, and Hannington's guards begin to strip him of his clothing. He is quite passive in their hands.
He has commended his soul to Him who sits
above kings. 'Tell the king,'—he is reported to have said,—'that I die for Uganda.
I have bought this road with my life.'

"They had now forced him to his knees.
Then the spears are flung into that heart
which had overflowed with such fervent
love for his murderers and their race. The
warriors with a wild cry now spring upon
the defenseless porters, and soon the fright-
ful butchery is accomplished; and then, as
if half fearing what they had done, the

"Tell the King That I Die for Uganda"

army of the Busoga and Waganda murderers hurries away, leaving the dead lying where they had fallen. Night draws her curtain over the scene, and when the moon comes out, she shines peacefully upon the seeming sleepers."

For several weeks after the tragedy was past, the missionaries in Uganda receiving conflicting reports about what had happened, lived with a faint hope that the bishop was still alive. If he had been murdered, they expected that any day they themselves, like their bishop, would be summoned forth to die; yet they quietly went about their usual work as if nothing had happened. Although the missionaries knew it not, day after day, the king and chiefs assembled to discuss the question whether or not Mr. Ashe, Mr. O'Flaherty, and Mr. Mackay should be killed. At last the dread decision was made, Mwanga's word was given. The three Englishmen must die.

The king's chief storekeeper, however, being a Christian, quietly sent word to the missionaries suggesting that they send a present to the king. Nalumasi, a Christian princess, one of Mwanga s sisters, also sent word warning them that if ever they needed to gain the good will of Mwanga it was then. The Roman Catholic priests also sent messengers to say that there was no longer a doubt about the bishop's murder, and that Mwanga had determined to kill Mr. Ashe, Mr. O'Flaherty, and Mr. Mackay, too.

So the missionaries gathered together about twenty loads of their most valuable possessions and sent them as presents to the king, the katikiro, and one of the most important chiefs. The next morning a large band of pages came to the mission with the command from the king for Mackay to go at once to the palace. What did it mean? Was there some new danger to face? The missionaries knelt to pray. Then manfully Mr. Ashe and Mr. Mackay went before the king.

The conversation opened by Mwanga's

saying: "What is the meaning of the present you sent me?"

"For friendship," answered Mackay.

"Have I 'eaten Uganda' only to-day (Have I come to the throne to-day)? Why give it to me now, and not long ago?"

Some talk followed concerning a gun Mackay had been repairing. Then Mwanga returned to his first question. "Well now, the present, what is it for?"

"We thought you were angry with us, because when we came to see you, you refused to see us," was Mackay's reply.

"Yes," broke in one of the chiefs, "they sent me a present, and the katikiro also, because they think we can influence the king. They think we want to kill them, and they wish to redeem their lives. What danger are they in? Do we kill guests?"

Mr. Mackay, turning to him, merely said, "Why, then, did you send back to say your present was not large enough, and to tell us to send you more?"

At this the others smiled a little and the

chief had nothing more to say. Yet they all began to rail on the two white men.

At last Mackay said, "Have we done wrong to give the king a present?" It was a telling question and again they were silent.

Then Mr. Ashe spoke: "You all know why we sent it. We want to hear about our brother."

"Who told you about your brother?" every one cried.

"Does not all Uganda know it?"

"Oh, do all Uganda go to your place?"

Then the king, turning to one of the chiefs, said, "Question them exceedingly."

So the two men were mercilessly plied with questions. The king wanted the names of the men who had told them of the plot. The missionaries refused to give any names. The chiefs grew angry. The king called the white men *"bagwagwa,"* the most insulting name in the Luganda language. The more quiet the missionaries were, the more angry grew the king and chiefs.

230

"What if I kill you?" cried Mwanga, "What would Queeni (the Queen) do? Was she able to touch Lukonge or Mirambo when they killed white men? What could she do, or all Europe together? How could they come—would they fly?"

This mocking and jeering and taunting continued for more than two hours until the missionaries were thoroughly worn out.

Mwanga made the threat that he would arrest and kill the white men if any Waganda were found on their premises, whether the white men knew it or not, and the "readers" also would lose their lives.

Then suddenly he called an attendant and cried, "Take these white men and give them two cows to quiet their minds," and with a wave of his hand he dismissed the court. Mr. Mackay and Mr. Ashe returned to their home thankful to God that he had given them strength to be true to him in the midst of such trying conditions.

That very night, regardless of Mwanga's threat, word came to the missionaries from a group of Christians gathered in the home of Nua, the head blacksmith for the king, saying that five persons wanted to be baptized. One of these five men was Gabunga, the admiral of the king's fleet of canoes on Victoria Lake. "So it is, and ever will be," wrote Mr. Mackay, "some will press into the kingdom in times of the greatest trial."

For about six months there was a lull in the storm. At this time of quiet Mr. O'Flaherty received permission from the king to leave the country. Worn and broken in health by frequent attacks of fever, he turned his face toward the shores of his beloved England. While his vessel sped on its way northward, he breathed his last, and his body, like those of many homeward-bound voyagers before him, found its resting-place in the ocean.

Ever since Bishop Hannington's martyrdom, Mwanga had acted like a criminal ever fearing arrest. He was too proud to admit his guilt, yet afraid that the white men and their followers would one day rob him of his kingdom. As long as he was willing to listen to some show of reason, the fact that the number of Christians had grown so large restrained him from ordering their wholesale massacre. Indeed, the katikiro had advised Mwanga to kill all who had learned to read; but the king said that all his pages, guards, and servants were "readers," that about five hundred men and boys and as many women and girls went to the Englishmen to learn, and about the same number to the Frenchmen. If he killed them all at once, he would be accused of killing the whole country; therefore, he would kill them a few at a time.

A number of events, each small in itself, served to stir up Mwanga's illtemper until all the evil of the boy-tyrant's nature seemed to break loose in a furious passion for murder. One bold lad, Balikudembe, formerly a pupil of Mackay's, dared to accuse his majesty of wrong-doing in killing the bishop, since the white men were the country's friends.

233

"This fellow has insulted me," angrily cried Mwanga, and ordered that Balikudembe be burned alive.

The executioner, a friend of the boy, thought to delay in carrying out the sentence; but the katikiro, who hated Balikudembe because he was a Christian, sent word to the executioner to kill the fellow at once, before the king had time to repent. Mwanga did repent afterward, and sent word to make the boy merely a prisoner. But it was too late. Brave Balikudembe had already gone where wicked rulers cease troubling.

Other events helped to irritate the already unhappy king. His straw-built hut, in which he kept his stores of gunpowder, caught fire, and a high wind carried the masses of blazing grass hither and yon among the other royal houses of the enclosure until his entire palace grounds had become a heap of ashes. He fled to the house of the katikiro only to have it shortly struck by lightning. Mwanga, crazed with

234

fear, thought that the god of lightning was his enemy and that he had been bewitched by the white men. Surely they had set fire to his stores of gunpowder, so that when the English army marched against his capital, he would have nothing with which to fight.

About this time, Mwanga ordered the mission boat to be brought to a certain place; in case Mackay obeyed the king, the executioner was ordered to be in waiting to put him to death. For once even the katikiro proved to be a friend of the white man. Through his timely warning, Mackay was enabled to escape the plot of the king and executioner.

From time to time disturbing reports reached the missionaries. Now it was the Uganda Christians who were to be seized; again it was the mission property which was to be plundered; sometimes their own lives were threatened. Mackay and Ashe lived and worked on not knowing when rumors might become realities.

235

May twenty-sixth, 1886, was bright of sky but dark of deed. Mr. Ashe with a company of "readers" about him, was seated on the porch at the back of the mission house. They had just been singing,

"All the people bow before Thee,
  Thou the Ruler of the heavens,"

when Mackay appeared suddenly. Speaking in English to Mr. Ashe, he said, "At last it is really true. I have just heard that Mwanga has gone mad and given orders to seize all the Christians."

"Escape quickly lest they search our place," said Mr. Ashe to the boys in Luganda; and skipping through a hole in the back fence, all the pupils soon disappeared. Scarcely had they gone, when an officer of the king arrived with a company of armed men in search for "readers," but none were found.

One of the Mwanga's own sisters had been bold enough to burn up her magic charms and ancestral relics. "The rebellion is

spreading even into my own household,"
thought Mwanga, "I must act quickly."
Soon by his command, so it was reported to
the missionaries, seventy of the leading
Christians were imprisoned.

One man, Alexandro by name, on hearing
that his fellow Christians were being arrested, went boldly to the king's court as
usual. "I myself am a Christian," was his
sturdy reply to the executioner's question
if any "readers" were hidden in his enclosure. Upon this faithful confession, Alexandro, too, was thrown into prison.

Two Christian young men, one Apolo
Kagwa by name, were called into the king's
presence. In a fit of madness, Mwanga
himself attacked one of them, gashing his
body fearfully with a spear, the suffering
man then being hurried off to the executioner.

Turning to Apolo Kagwa, Mwanga cried,
"Are you a reader?"

"I read, my lord," was the heroic reply.
"Then I'll teach you to read!" and thus

shouting, the furious king, with spear in hand, wounded and bruised the body of the faithful Christian. Yet Kagwa's life was spared.

While "readers" were being hunted like wild beasts, many of them fled to distant provinces. Some refused to hide, lest their enemies might accuse them of being cowards. One such was Roberto, who had been accustomed almost daily to come to the mission. Mackay knew him well, since together they had made several trips to and from the southern end of the lake.

As Roberto with a group of boys about him was one day enjoying a quiet prayer-meeting, he was surprised to discover two or three executioners standing outside the door of his hut. Immediately, all his boys except one bolted through the reed partition wall and escaped. A gun was leaning against the door, and seeing this the executioners hesitated to enter.

"Do not be afraid that I will shoot," said Roberto, "come in and take me."

Binding him and the one boy with him, the executioners dragged the two before the king.

"Do you read?" asked his majesty.

"Yes."

"Take him and roast him," was the tyrant's fiendish reply.

The boy's life was redeemed by friends who gave the king in return a woman and a cow. Roberto was kept in the stocks for a few days, and then was led forth to his death. His bleeding body, mercilessly mangled with the sword, was thrown into the flames.

Another who refused to flee was Nua, head blacksmith to the king. While laboring with Mackay over the coffin for Mutesa's mother, he had become a friend of the white man. Later, Nua became a Christian and indeed an elder in the Waganda church. In times of peril, he had faithfully invited the Christians to gather in his home. On hearing of the arrests, he hurried his wife and children and two or three Christian boys who had been living with him off to a place of hiding. For himself, he refused to flee, and of course was arrested.

While bound hand and foot in prison, he pleaded with the executioners to become Christians. Noticing among those who were imprisoned with him one who had been arrested for cattle-stealing, Nua asked the executioner not to kill the cattle-stealer along with the Christians. The matter was reported to Mwanga, and the cattle-stealer was pardoned; but Nua and his Christian companions were burned alive.

The day after the arrest of the seventy Christians, the alarming report reached the missionaries that their houses were to be plundered. All the white men's Waganda servants and boys were immediately dismissed, and Mr. Mackay and Mr. Ashe were left alone in their enclosure. To them it was indeed a dark day.

"What anguish of soul we have experienced," wrote Mr. Mackay, "no words can express. Let some of our friends at home fancy themselves exchanging places with us, and seeing their friends, with whom they yesterday talked and ate and prayed, to-day ruthlessly seized and hacked to pieces almost before their eyes, and their members left lying to decay by the roadside."

"Something must be done," they said. "We must at least make an attempt to save the lives of those who are imprisoned but not yet killed."

So, as soon as possible, Mackay hurried to Mwanga's court. On being presented to the king, he reminded his majesty that, for a piece of work the missionary had previously done, Mwanga had promised to give him anything he would like.

The king graciously renewed the promise and asked, "What do you want?"

"I want the lives of the people whom you have seized and not yet killed."

Mwanga, somewhat taken back by this request, tried to excuse himself from keeping the promise by saying, "But they are already all dead."

241

"No," said Mackay, "there are many still alive."

"Well, there may be five or six or even ten," said Mwanga, "they shall not be killed."

Mackay begged that the executioner be summoned at once and given the new order. This was not done, however, the king insisting that he had already given orders to spare several, and all the others were dead.

But Mwanga's promises were worthless. Only a few days later, thirty-two of the imprisoned Christians were killed, having been thrown together in one great pile and burned alive. After the deed was done, the head executioner said to Mwanga that he had never before killed men who showed such bravery and calmness in the face of death.

"In the fire, they even prayed aloud to God," he said.

During the weeks and months which followed, the missionaries' headquarters were watched by the executioners. More "read-

ers" were captured and killed; and scores
and even hundreds went into hiding. The
missionaries saw little of their Waganda
friends. Occasionally they would be awakened in the middle of the night by one or
two of the bolder Christians who under the
cover of darkness would venture out.

Strange to say, at this most dangerous
time, some even asked for baptism. One of
these was a pupil of Roberto, the Christian who refused to protect himself by using his gun. Mr. Ashe being the preacher,
the boy went to him and said, "My friend,
I wish to be baptized."

"Do you know what you are asking?"
Mr. Ashe said in surprise.

"I know, my friend."

"But you know that if you say you are a
Christian they will kill you?"

Again the boy answered the same words,
"I know, my friend."

"But suppose people ask you if you are
a reader, will you tell a lie and deny it and
say 'No?'"

243

"I shall confess, my friend."

Mr. Mackay and Mr. Ashe, having known the boy for some time and believing him to be a true Christian, consented to his baptism.

At three o'clock one morning, while it was still very dark, Mr. Ashe was awakened by a low knocking at his door. Arising and lighting his lamp, he recognized almost half a dozen Christian men standing in front of the house, and he invited them in. One of them, Samweli by name, was in great trouble and had come to ask advice. Since he was among the best known of the Christians, he had been hunted most carefully by the executioners. Being away in a distant province, gathering tribute for the king, he had escaped. But now he had returned. His companions had urged him to flee, but he could not feel that it was right for him not to deliver the tribute of cowry-shells to the king; yet to show himself at the palace would mean almost certain death. What was he to do?

Mr. Ashe's advice was soon given. He said, "The king has not the heart of a man, but of a wild beast, and you are not bound to submit yourself to one who is so vile a murderer. You are perfectly justified in forsaking the trust."

They stepped over to Mr. Mackay's shop and he, too, advised Samweli to flee. But the heroic Waganda Christian was not satisfied. For some time he sat on the earthen floor of the room looking much troubled. Finally he asked for a pencil and paper and bent over as if to write.

"You need not write; but tell me what you think," said Mr. Ashe.

Then, looking up, he said to the missionary, "My friend, I cannot leave the things of the king."

His companions began to try to show him the folly of his decision, but Mr. Ashe said, "No, he is right; he has spoken well; he must take the tribute."

After kneeling together in prayer, they planned that Samweli should deliver the cowry-shells to the appointed chief very early in the morning, and perhaps the executioners would not yet be abroad in search of Christians. When Samweli said good-by to the missionaries, they had little hope of seeing his face again. How thankful they were when at nightfall, he appeared once more at the mission, happy because he had done his duty, even though at the risk of life itself.

Late one night in June, two Christians, one of them for the third time fleeing for his life, visited the mission. To these men, Mr. Mackay and Mr. Ashe gave a letter which they had written for circulation among the Christians in hiding. Like some of Paul's letters to his persecuted followers, how it must have cheered many a lonely convert! It read:

" PEOPLE OF JESUS WHO ARE IN UGANDA

"Our Friends:—We, your friends and teachers, write to you to send you words of cheer and comfort, which we have taken from the Epistle of Peter, the apostle of

Christ. In days of old, Christians were hated, were hunted, were driven out, and were persecuted for Jesus' sake; and thus it is to-day.

"Our beloved brethren, do not deny our Lord Jesus, and he will not deny you on that great day when he shall come with glory. Remember the words of our Saviour, how he told his disciples not to fear men, who are able to kill only the body; but he bade them to fear God, who is able to destroy the body together with the soul.

"Do not cease to pray exceedingly, and to pray for our brothers who are in affliction, and for those who do not know God. May God give you his Spirit and his blessing! May he deliver you out of all your afflictions! May he give you entrance to eternal life through Jesus Christ our Saviour!

"Farewell. We are the white men; we are your brothers indeed who have written to you."

On the other side of the letter was written the fourth chapter of the First Letter of Peter, from the twelfth verse to the end of the chapter.

So in Uganda the native Christians, not long since degraded heathen, were now suffering torment and death rather than deny their Lord and Saviour. In all, about two hundred Protestant and Roman Catholic converts were brought to a cruel martyrdom, and probably more than that number were made exiles from their homes.

It was in like manner that centuries ago, in the days of Nero at Rome, the early Christians suffered. So some of our own forefathers were burned at the stake. So in later years the Christian churches in Madagascar, the Hawaiian Islands, Japan, and China have added to the noble company of martyrs.

Like the faithful heroes told of in the eleventh chapter of Hebrews, they were "tortured, not accepting their deliverance; that they might obtain a better resurrection: and others had trial of mockings and

248

scourgings, yea, moreover of bonds and imprisonment: they were stoned, they were sawn asunder, they were tempted, they were slain with the sword: . . . being destitute, afflicted, ill-treated, (of whom the world was not worthy), wandering in deserts and mountains and caves, and the holes of the earth.'' ''But now they desire a better country, that is, a heavenly: wherefore God is not ashamed of them, to be called their God; for he hath prepared for them a city.''

CHAPTER XII

THE WHITE MAN OF WORK LAYS DOWN HIS TOOLS

ONCE more there was a period of comparative quiet in Uganda. Another of the white men left for England. Indeed, Mr. Ashe and Mr. Mackay had both asked permission to go. This was not because of any thought of abandoning their work nor because of any fear of death. But it was thought that perhaps through their temporary absence the persecutions of the Christians might cease. Then being again quiet in mind, Mwanga might with real heartiness invite the missionaries to return to his capital.

After many discussions at court, his black majesty finally consented that Mr. Ashe should leave, but not so Mr. Mackay, for whom the king pretended to have a most remarkable affection. So Mr. Mackay bade farewell to his long-time companion, and for nearly a year held the fort in Uganda alone.

Notwithstanding the edict that all who dared to go to the mission would be put to death, large numbers of "readers" stole away unnoticed to the white man's house. Several months after Mr. Ashe left, Mr. Mackay wrote:

"For a couple of months after you left I was having a regular houseful of strangers every evening. The tin of petroleum arrived in time, and with it I could make a respectable light, so that the library became a night-school. Late, late, often very late, we wound up, and I was often more than exhausted—reading, teaching, giving medicine, and doing other work. By day I got, off and on, some translation done."

In addition to his teaching and doctoring, the "white man of work" undertook to construct a spinning-wheel and weaver's loom so that the Waganda might learn to spin and to weave their own cloth.

When the royal mechanics had all failed, Mackay was asked to mount a huge flagstaff in the king's enclosure. Very awkward helpers they were who aided him, and it was only after many days of patient labor that the pole slipped into the hole dug for it, and stood up tall and firm, to the astonishment and delight of the king and chiefs.

Whenever time could be spared, Mackay labored on the translation and printing of the Gospel of Matthew. In a few months the first edition of one hundred and fifty copies came from the press, and the eager Christians were able to read for themselves the precious stories of the Christ;—his coming as a babe in Bethlehem, his teachings on the Mount, his miracles, his parables, and finally his sufferings, death, and resurrection.

But such events as these came only occasionally to brighten Mackay's life. For the most part the shadows far outnumbered the bright spots throughout that year of loneliness. Again and again plots were laid for his life; and since the fickle Mwanga could never be trusted, much of Mackay's work had to be done in secret. In dangers oft and trials ever, how hard it must have been to keep brave and cheerful! In a letter written about this time Mackay said:

"What sadness and melancholy comes over me at times, and I find myself shedding tears like a child! Then those wonderfully consoling Psalms send a thrill of joy into my whole being.

"I have not the slightest desire to 'escape,' if I can do a particle of good by staying. My desire is that the Lord will open the way for the mission to be kept up, not abandoned. Our ship is in port, some twelve miles off, and possibly I might make a dash for it; but what then? I do not at present see that I am warranted in seeking to do so. Anything may happen at any moment, and it may be that I shall be led to adopt such a course; but hitherto I believe

I am doing right in quietly going on with the work. My earnest heart-wish is simply to cast myself on the Master, and say, 'Thy will be done!'"

For a time Mwanga pretended to be a Mohammedan, and ordered all his pages to read the Koran. On the refusal of a number to obey his orders, Mwanga complained that all those who read with the white men were stubborn and compelled him to be ever killing them, so that people would call him a madman! He threatened to "kill very many." But his queenmother, although a heathen, warned him against putting his pages to death; since, she said, in a few years they would be the chief strength of his country.

Now that Mackay was alone, his old enemies, the Arabs, redoubled their efforts to drive him from the country. Again and again they slandered his character before Mwanga. When a letter, written in Arabic, came from the English consul in Zanzibar, they mistranslated it to the king, so that it read that the consul advised Mwanga to drive Mackay out of the country at once. The king hesitated, not knowing which to believe, the Arabs or Mackay. Now, he seemed to favor Mackay's leaving; again, he refused his permission. The strain of uncertainty lasted several weeks, but Mackay waited in patience.

Finally the king definitely declared: "I will not have his teaching in the country while I live. After I am dead the people may learn to read."

Mackay did not leave, however, until he gained a promise from the king to send a native messenger along with him in the boat, so that, on the return trip of the ship, another Englishman might be brought to Uganda to take Mackay's place.

So one day in the summer of 1887, Mackay bade farewell to his Uganda home, and to the great heathen capital and its king, locked up the mission houses, and started for the port.

Good-by gifts were given back and forth

between Mwanga, the chiefs, and Mackay;
and the Waganda Christians called to have
their last words with the white man. For
nine years he had been to some of them a
faithful friend and father, and it was hard
for them to let him go.

Not long, however, were the persecuted
Waganda Christians left alone. The boat
that carried Mr. Mackay to the southern
end of the lake brought Mr. Gordon, a
nephew of Bishop Hannington, to take his
place. Mr. Gordon was soon joined by Mr.
Walker, and these two brave men persistently kept the work moving forward.

Within about a year's time two revolutions occurred in Uganda. Mwanga's
cruelties grew so loathsome to his subjects
that they arose in a body and dethroned
him, placing his brother, Kalema, on the
throne in his stead. Under the new monarch, Roman Catholic and Protestant
Christians were given the chief offices of
the kingdom, and, for a while, "readers"
flocked to the mission like "swarms of

bees." The jealousy of the Arabs, however, was not long in being stirred. They headed a second revolution. A new king was put on the throne, and the important chieftainships given to Mohammedans.

For six days both the French and English missionaries were imprisoned in a filthy hut within the king's enclosure. The furious Mohammedan mob robbed the Protestant mission of every article of furniture, beds, tables, chairs, book-cases, boxes, everything. "Every book was torn to bits," and every bottle of medicine was smashed or emptied of its contents. Doors were wrenched from their hinges and carried away, and the mission house left a desolate wreck.

The French priests and Protestant missionaries were together put on board the white man's ship, no food, almost no clothing, and no bedding being allowed for their voyage to the southern end of the lake. Mr. Walker was even robbed of his hat, coat, and trousers before starting, and the only two books he had saved, his New Testament and prayer-book, were snatched from him and thrown into the lake.

"The captain carried us on board," wrote Mr. Gordon, "and we heard the voice of the officer behind us. He was giving us Uganda's parting message. 'Let no white man come to Uganda for the space of two years. We do not want to see Mackay's boat in Uganda waters for a long time to come. We do not want to see a white teacher back again in Uganda until we have converted the whole of Uganda to the Mohammedan faith'."

While revolutions and fanatical outbursts were taking place in Uganda, Mackay was beginning missionary work anew at a place called Usambiro, near the southern shore of Victoria Lake.

About seventy miles to the eastward, a wretched fugitive, having escaped from Uganda in a canoe with perhaps half a dozen companions, was the cruel, despised Mwanga. Regardless of the unspeakable wrongs this tyrant had committed against him and against so many whom he loved, the earnest, forgiving missionary now wrote and offered the ruined king a refuge with him in Usambiro.

" Murderer and persecutor as he has been," wrote Mr. Mackay, "I yet have not the faintest doubt that it becomes us to do everything in our power to return him good for evil."

Mwanga, fearing the Arabs, felt at the time unable to escape. He implored Mackay to come to him to deliver him, but this the missionary could not do. Some months later, Mwanga fled to the Catholic mission where he was soon baptized. By a third revolution in Uganda, he was later restored to his throne, and the chieftainships were divided equally between the Christians and Arabs; but Mwanga was as Samson with his hair shorn. Never again did he gain his old power. He became little more than a puppet in the hands of his chiefs, and at his death no one could say that he had ever shown any certain signs

259

that he had become a real heart-Christian.

In the meantime, what was Mackay doing at Usambiro? When the Waganda Christians were exiled from their country, some twenty-five of them fled to Mackay. With their assistance, he built a neat five-room house for himself and the two or three other white men who sometimes were with him. Workshops, houses for his boys, buildings for his chickens, goats, and cattle, and a garden where he could raise vegetables were other results of their industry. Finally, the entire grounds, when enclosed by a neat grass fence, became an attractive homelike spot in the midst of a barren, dry, and treeless waste.

Even when driven from Uganda, Mackay did not cease to toil for the land he had long since called his own. He directed his exiled Christians in the use of the printing-press, and many pages of Scripture verses, prayers, and hymns from time to time were sent to Uganda. Then, too, with the assistance of the more intelligent among the

Christians, he began the translation of the Gospel according to St. John.

For years it had been his ambition to build a good steam launch for the use of the missionaries on Victoria Lake. Indeed, on first coming to Africa he brought with him a steam-boiler and engine, but he had never succeeded in gaining Mutesa's or Mwanga's permission to build the boat. Now, at last he was able to begin. Writing home, he said:

"I have my hands full, preparing to build our new boat. I have cut the timber some twenty miles distant, and have carried it here. You will be probably disgusted at hearing that I am busy just now making bricks to build a house in which to build the vessel. Within the last fortnight we have made some ten thousand. That is doubtless poor work to be occupied with in the mission field, but it must be done; and even in such a humble occupation I hope the good Lord will not withhold his blessing. Mission boats unfortunately do not grow

261

of themselves—they have to be built, every inch of them. But trees have been growing for ages, of the Lord's planting; and as we fell them, I like to think that he made them grow for this purpose."

A little later he wrote again: "I have just received seventy loads of rivets, fittings, rope, paint, and other material, for this vessel, for which I am collecting the needed timber. Some time ago I wrote you of my felling trees in the forest some ten to twenty miles distant. The problem then was to have these conveyed to this station. I found that the logs were too heavy either to drag or to have carried by all the men I could muster. I therefore set to work and made a strong four-wheeled wagon with which to fetch the logs entire here. This has proved quite a success, and already we have dragged a log weighing a ton and a half to this place with no difficulty. It is the first wheeled vehicle ever seen in this region since the world began, with the exception of an iron wheelbarrow which was used in the building of the Suez Canal, and was shipped over here. This wheelbarrow has proved a marvel to the natives; but the ease with which our wagon rolls along with a large log on the top of it, is a far greater wonder still.''

It was in August, 1889, the last summer of Mackay's life. Mr. Stanley happened to be returning to the coast, having rescued an English governor who had long been held a prisoner in Central Africa. Passing by Mackay's mission, he and his company remained with the missionary nearly a month. Stanley's story of his visit gives a picture of the kind of life Mackay was living.

"The next day," says Mr. Stanley, "having already sent messages ahead, that we might not take Mr. Mackay by surprise, we arrived in view of the English mission. It was built in the middle of what appeared to be no better than a gray waste. The ground gently sloped from curious heaps of big boulders, or enormous blocks thrown higgeledy-piggledy to the height of a respec-

table hill, down to a marshy flat, green with
its dense crop of papyrus. Beyond this we
saw a gleam of a line of water, produced
from an inlet of Victoria Lake. We were
approaching the mission by a wagon track,
and presently we came to the wagon itself,
a simple thing of wooden wheels, for carrying timber for building. There was not a
green thing in view, except in the marsh;
grass all dead, trees either shrunk, with-
ered, or dead,—at least there was not the
promise of a bud anywhere, which of course
was entirely due to the dry season.

"When we were about half a mile off,
a gentleman of small stature, with brown
hair, dressed in white linen and a gray hat,
advanced to meet us.

" 'And so you are Mr. Mackay? Mwanga
did not get you then, this time? What experiences you must have had with that man!
But you look so well, one would say you had
been to England lately.'

" 'Oh, no; this is my twelfth year.
Mwanga permitted me to leave, and the

"Talking Thus, We Entered the Circle of Tall Poles"

Rev. Cyril Gordon took my place; but not for long, since they were all shortly after expelled from Uganda.'

"Talking thus, we entered the circle of tall poles, within which the mission station was built. There were signs of labor, and constant unwearying patience and sweating under a hot sun. We saw that Mackay was determined to do something to keep the mind employed, and never to let idleness find him with folded hands brooding over the unloveliness.

"There was a big, solid workshop in the yard, filled with machinery and tools, a launch's boiler was being prepared by the blacksmiths, a big canoe was outside repairing; there were sawpits and large logs of hard timber; there were great stacks of palisade poles; in the corner of an outer yard was a cattle-fold and a goat-pen, fowls by the score pecked at minute grains; and out of the European quarter there trooped out a number of little boys and big boys, looking uncommonly sleek and

265

happy; and quiet laborers came up to bid us, with hats off, 'Good morning!'

"I was ushered into the room of a substantial clay structure, the walls about two feet thick, evenly plastered, and garnished with missionary pictures.

"There were four separate ranges of shelves filled with choice, useful books. 'Allah ho Akbar,' replied Hassan, his Zanzibar head-man, to me; 'books! Mackay has thousands of books, in the dining-room, bedroom, the church, everywhere. Books! ah, loads upon loads of them!' And while I was sipping real coffee, and eating home-made bread and butter for the first time for thirty months, I thoroughly sympathized with Mackay's love of books. It becomes quite clear why, among so many books and children and out-door work, Mackay cannot find leisure to brood and think of being lonely. He has no time to fret and groan and weep, and God knows if ever man had reason to be doleful and lonely and sad, Mackay had, when, after murdering his

266

bishop, and burning his pupils, and strangling his converts, and clubbing to death his dark friends, Mwanga turned his eye of death on him. And yet the little man met it with calm blue eyes that never winked. It is worth going a long journey to see one man of this kind, working day after day for twelve hours bravely, and without a syllable of complaint or a moan, and to hear him lead his little flock in singing and prayer to show forth God's kindness in the morning, and his faithfulness every night."

Stanley and his officers urged Mackay to return home with them; the Church Missionary Society secretaries, time after time, had invited him to return to England; his friends wrote letters begging him to come home for a rest; but the faithful Christian soldier refused to leave his post until more men were sent to carry on the work in his absence.

At last, only a few months later, his summons to rest came from his Lord in heaven. His only white companion in Usambiro, Mr.

Deekes, was preparing to return to England because of ill health. The day of his departure came. He and his men had risen early and all the packing which was still to be done was completed by sunrise, and they were ready to start on the long march to the coast.

But where was Mr. Mackay? Could it be that he was sleeping while the others within the enclosure were up and busy helping the party get a good start before the scorching sun compelled them to halt? Mr. Mackay had worked hard the day before and perhaps he was resting unusually soundly. Expecting to say good-by to his faithful friend, Mr. Deekes entered Mackay's room. When he returned to his men, he dismissed them and ordered all preparations for the march to cease, for Mackay was lying on his bed burning with fever.

During the whole day his Waganda boys with solemn, questioning faces flitted quietly about, doing their necessary duties. No doctor was near. Mr. Deekes himself was weak and could do little. The care of the sick missionary was left largely to untrained Waganda Christians who did the best they knew to cool his fevered brow. During the next four days Mr. Mackay, in his delirium, knew not the loving black nurses who, in their simple way were doing their utmost to win their beloved teacher back to life; but his spirit would not be detained. His Master called, "Enter thou into the joy of thy Lord," and Alexander Mackay was gone.

"I had a coffin made of the wood he had cut for the boat," wrote Mr. Deekes, "and at two o'clock in the afternoon on Sunday I buried him by the side of the late Bishop Parker. The Waganda Christians and the boys of the village stood around the grave, and I began to read the burial service, but broke down with grief and weakness. The boys and Waganda Christians sang the hymn, 'All hail the power of Jesus' name,' in Luganda, and we returned to the house, never to forget that day."

269

So it was that Africa lost the man whom Stanley called "the best missionary since Livingstone."

DID IT PAY?

ALEXANDER MACKAY was only forty-one years of age when he was called to lay aside his life-work. When a young man he might have turned a deaf ear to Stanley's urgent call from Central Africa and remained in merry England, where fever is as little to be feared as are lions and rhinoceri. Had he done so, who knows but that he might have lived out a long life of twice forty-one years.

He might have continued his work in Germany, perhaps coming to be a famous engineer or inventor. Having been offered a position with good opportunities for promotion in the service of the Imperial East Africa Company, he might have become a prosperous business man. General Gordon had wanted him as an important officer in his army in Egypt. Had he accepted the offer, perhaps he might have ended his life as one of Great Britain's well-known commanders. Instead, he died in the prime of life—a missionary in remote Central Africa.

Fourteen years in Africa had brought to Mr. Mackay the knottiest of problems and hardships untold. During all this time, luxury was far from him, and often he lacked even what we regard as common comforts. No mother or sister or wife was at his side to brighten his simple home. Late and early, he toiled, ofttimes at tasks for which he had no special liking. Many of those whom he had so patiently taught and whom he had come to love as his own brothers, he saw sent to cruel torture and death. For months at a time he lived knowing not when a wicked monarch might call for his life.

His has not been the only promising life laid down for Uganda. In 1876, seven others besides Mackay had left their homes

in answer to King Mutesa's plea. During
the years since then, scores of other young
men and even some women, just as earnest
and devoted to the work and to their Lord
as Mackay, have started for the shores of
Victoria Lake. Some have died on the
way; others have lived for only a short time
in the land of their choice; and a few have
survived to do many years of patient service. But has it all been worth while? Did
it pay?

It was a letter from a newspaper correspondent published in the London *Telegraph* that first led Christian teachers to
give their lives for Uganda. Twenty-nine
years later another newspaper correspondent wrote a letter from Uganda's capital,
and this was published in the London *Times*
for August 11, 1904. Unlike Stanley, this
second newspaper man had in a few days
traveled by railroad from the east coast of
Africa to Victoria Lake. On board a beautiful modern lake steamer, he had sailed to
Uganda's port. He found a people gov-

erned by a Christian king whose noble prime
minister was Apolo Kagwa, once persecuted,
and now one of the pillars of the Waganda
Christian Church. He found a country under the protection of the English crown,
ruled by just laws, and a nation wholly
without slaves. He found that only a few
of its citizens still brought their offerings
to the heathen spirits, and those few seemed
half ashamed to be thought of as believers
in the wizards. Thousands of people, he
found, belonged to the churches which had
been organized all over the country.

It was one day the privilege of this newspaper correspondent to see more than five
thousand of these Waganda Christians
gathered at the capital. His letter tells the
story of the great occasion.

"On the summit of Namirembe has stood
for many years the principal Christian
church of Uganda, a large building, the
grass roof of which was supported by a
very forest of palm poles. This eventually
became unsafe, and has lately been replaced

274

by a more permanent and really beautiful building, which reflects great credit on Mr. Borup, an engineer missionary. He has taught the Waganda to make bricks, has instructed young men in carpentry and other handicrafts, and has superintended this their first building on a large scale. The walls and two rows of massive columns are built of sun-dried bricks, while those used for the foundations have been burnt in a kiln. The roof, neatly thatched with long grass, rises over the transepts into three peaks. But the most remarkable features in the building are the beautiful reed-work which covers the ceiling and the palm stems that serve as beams and rafters.

"The great event in the capital recently has been the consecration of this cathedral by Bishop Tucker. At five in the morning of the twenty-first of June, people were beginning to assemble in the open space around the church. The service was to begin at nine o'clock, but long before that hour every available space had been filled and the

great building was surrounded by a large
crowd of disappointed but cheerful and orderly people who found it impossible to gain
admission.

"The seats were a few reserved for Eu-
ropeans under the central dome and those
kept for the clergy in the chancel; all the
rest of the floor space, with the exception of
the central aisle and well-kept passages to
the different doorways, was completely covered by rows of Waganda seated on the
ground, or on skins and mats which many
had brought with them. No undue crowd-
ing had been allowed; but by this method of
seating, any given space will accommodate
a considerably larger number of people
than it takes where room has to be found for
chairs or benches. Looking down from the
chancel, the eye wandered over a sea of dark
but by no means unattractive faces, and one
noticed a marked contrast between the two
sides of the church, for to the right sat the
men in their clean, long white robes, and to
the left the women, clad for the most part in
276

the rich brown bark cloth so characteristic of Uganda."

King Daudi Chwa, Apolo Kagwa, the prime minister, and about fifty missionaries and native pastors from all parts of the kingdom and a vast congregation of 3,500 within the cathedral listened reverently through the entire services.

"The building of the cathedral had involved a considerable drain upon the resources of the people, and there still remained a debt of more than 2,000 rupees [$650]. To meet this was the object of the collection taken up toward the end of the proceedings, and a most interesting part of the ceremony it proved to be. Quite a little army of men were employed going to and fro with large bags and cloths, and they returned again and again to the chancel heavily laden with strings of cowry-shells, besides the more regular coinage introduced with British rule. These were received by the clergy in the basin-shaped baskets that figure largely in native life. Many brought

277

offerings in kind, and the English section of
the congregation could not repress their
smiles when the first chicken was solemnly
carried up the aisle and deposited at the
foot of the table, followed almost immediately by a couple of goats which showed a
marked objection to being dragged back and
removed by a side door. It then appeared
that gifts were flowing in, not only from
the congregation proper, but from the yet
greater crowd which had failed to gain admission and thronged around the building
outside all through the service. Load after
load of offerings came through the doors,
and many were the gifts that did not appear within. Others arrived too late for
the occasion, and the amount of the collection went on growing for days afterward.
The latest figures I could obtain were as follows: 1,613 rupees [$538], including
about 90,000 shells, and 36 bullocks and
cows, 23 goats, 31 fowls, and 154 eggs. The
result of this collection more than wiped off
the debt on the church.

"Load after Load of Offerings Came Through the Doors"

"Altogether the scene described was never to be forgotten by an English visitor. Less than thirty years ago, Stanley gave to the king of Uganda his first lesson in the truths of Christianty, and then appealed for missionaries to carry on the work. He lived to see a truly marvelous change effected by the preaching of the gospel, which is to-day being carried by native teachers and preachers far into the surrounding countries; and now within a few weeks of his death a gathering of over 5,000 Waganda for the consecration of a cathedral in Mutesa's capital witnesses to the force with which the Christian message can appeal to an intelligent people who have heard it for the first time in the present generation."

Was it all worth while? Did it pay? Were the lives wasted or well invested which have made possible such changes in a country once heathen? "Whosoever," said Jesus, "would save his life shall lose it; and whosoever shall lose his life for my sake and the gospel's shall save it."

INDEX

281

INDEX

283

INDEX